THE GREAT TREKS OF ENGLAND

Trekking the CLEVELAND WAY

by
Andrew
McCluggage

KNIFE EDGE
Outdoor Guidebooks

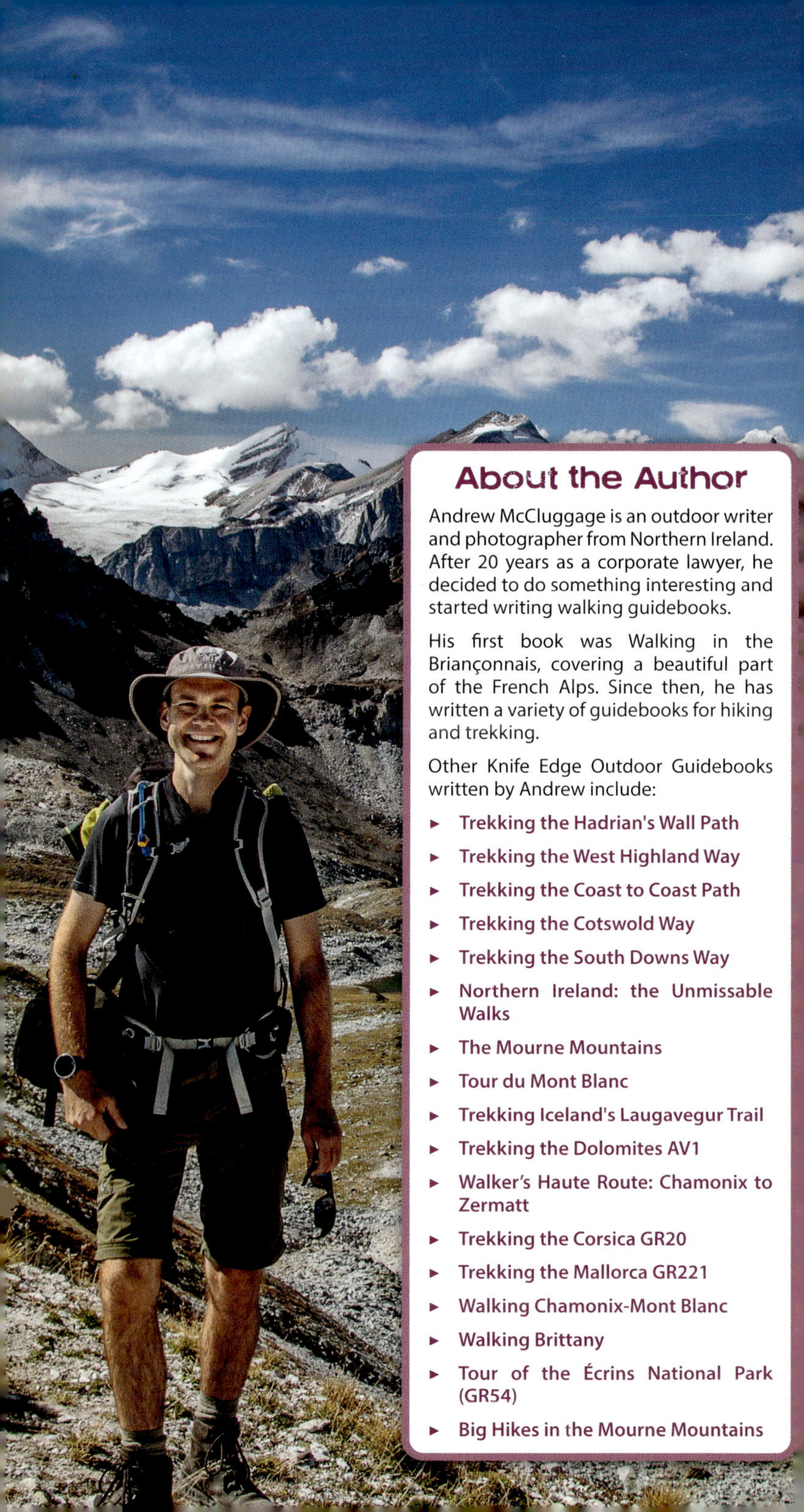

About the Author

Andrew McCluggage is an outdoor writer and photographer from Northern Ireland. After 20 years as a corporate lawyer, he decided to do something interesting and started writing walking guidebooks.

His first book was Walking in the Briançonnais, covering a beautiful part of the French Alps. Since then, he has written a variety of guidebooks for hiking and trekking.

Other Knife Edge Outdoor Guidebooks written by Andrew include:

- **Trekking the Hadrian's Wall Path**
- **Trekking the West Highland Way**
- **Trekking the Coast to Coast Path**
- **Trekking the Cotswold Way**
- **Trekking the South Downs Way**
- **Northern Ireland: the Unmissable Walks**
- **The Mourne Mountains**
- **Tour du Mont Blanc**
- **Trekking Iceland's Laugavegur Trail**
- **Trekking the Dolomites AV1**
- **Walker's Haute Route: Chamonix to Zermatt**
- **Trekking the Corsica GR20**
- **Trekking the Mallorca GR221**
- **Walking Chamonix-Mont Blanc**
- **Walking Brittany**
- **Tour of the Écrins National Park (GR54)**
- **Big Hikes in the Mourne Mountains**

Whitby's famous whale bone arch (Stage 7e/8)

KNIFE EDGE Outdoor Guidebooks

Publisher: Knife Edge Outdoor Limited (NI648568)
12 Torrent Business Centre, Donaghmore, County Tyrone, BT70 3BF, UK
www.knifeedgeoutdoor.com

ISBN: 978-1-912933-17-4

First edition 2024

A catalogue record for this book is available from the British Library

Front cover: The path along Hasty Bank (Stage 4)

Title page: The magnificent path above Loftus Alum Quarries (Stage 6b)

This page: The pier at Saltburn-by-the-Sea (Stage 5e/6a)

Back cover: One of the fabulous beaches along the Cleveland Way

Back cover flap: The village of Staithes (Stage 6b/7a)

All routes described in this book have been recently walked by the author and both the author and publisher have made all reasonable efforts to ensure that all information is as accurate as possible. However, while a printed book remains constant for the life of an edition, things in the countryside often change. Trails are subject to forces outside our control. For example, landslides, tree-falls or other matters can result in damage to paths or route changes; waymarks and signposts may fade or be destroyed by wind, snow or the passage of time; or trails may not be maintained by the relevant authorities. If you notice any discrepancies between the contents of this guide and the facts on the ground, then please let us know. Our contact details are listed at the back of this book.

Contents

The Repus (Stage 6a/6b)

Getting Help

Emergency services number: dial 999

Distress signal

The signal that you are in distress is 6 blasts on a whistle spaced over a minute, followed by a minute's silence. Then repeat. The acknowledgment that your signal has been received is 3 blasts of a whistle over a minute followed by a minute's silence. At night, flashes of a torch can also be used in the same sequences. **Always carry a torch and whistle.**

Signalling to a helicopter from the ground

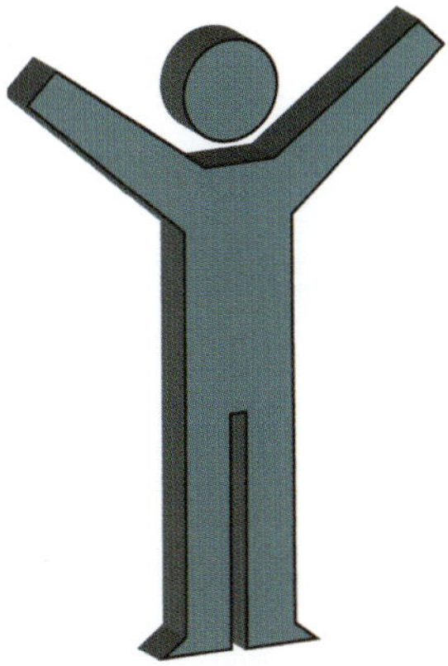

Help Required

Raise both arms in the shape of a 'Y'

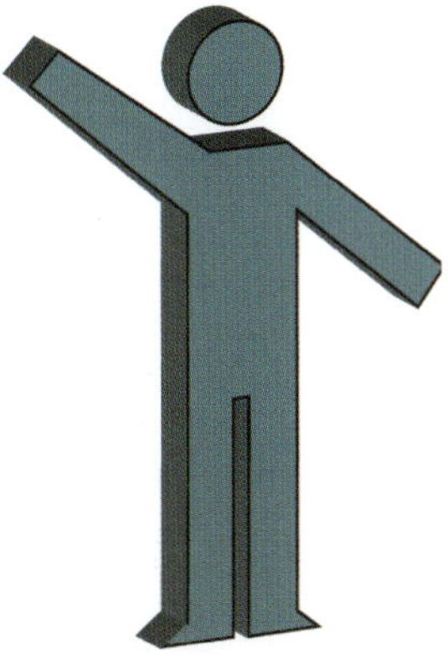

Help Not Required

Raise one arm and extend the other arm down and outwards

WARNING

Hills, cliffs and mountains can be dangerous places and walking is a potentially dangerous activity. Some of the routes described in this guide cross potentially hazardous terrain. You walk entirely at your own risk. It is solely your responsibility to ensure that you and all members of your group have adequate experience, fitness and equipment. Neither the author nor the publisher accepts any responsibility or liability whatsoever for death, injury, loss, damage or inconvenience resulting from use of this book, participation in the activity of mountain walking or otherwise.

Some land may be privately owned so we cannot guarantee that there is a legal right of entry to the land. Occasionally, routes change as a result of land disputes.

Runswick Bay (Stage 7c)

Introduction

The Wainstones (Stage 4)

After the success of the Pennine Way (which officially opened in 1965), the ribbon was cut for the Cleveland Way ('CLW') in 1969, making it the second trek in England to be designated as a 'National Trail'. At first glance, it may seem odd that the epic and notorious Pennine Way was followed up with a shorter and less well-known circuit in a remote corner of Northern England. However, those acquainted with the region would not have been surprised. They would have been familiar with the evocative expanses of the North York Moors, the sublime viewpoints on the escarpments of the Cleveland Hills, the seemingly never-ending cliffs of the Yorkshire coastline and the many quaint towns and villages that would welcome legions of hikers over the coming decades.

Even from a quick glance at a map of the CLW, you can see that it was cleverly devised to circumnavigate (almost entirely) the main body of the North York Moors National Park. On closer inspection, however, you will notice that the trek is divided into two very different parts, one inland and one coastal, enabling the hiker to explore the finest terrain that the park has to offer. The inland portion of the route is 58 miles long and visits a series of remote and beautiful moors as it travels the edge of the high escarpments on the W and N sides of the park: this is one of the largest expanses of heather moorland in the world and, because there are few trees, the far-reaching views are largely unimpeded. This landscape is at its finest in late summer when the heather blooms, covering the ground, as far as the eye can see, with a magnificent and unforgettable carpet of purple and pink. The birdlife is fabulous too with lapwing, curlew, grouse and many others nesting close to the path. You will not want to rush this wild terrain.

Although the transition between the two is rapid, the coastal section of the trek is a world apart from the moors. It follows the high cliffs of the Yorkshire coast for 52 miles, between the Victorian seaside resorts of Saltburn-by-the-Sea and Filey. Wonderful sea views are a constant companion. Each day, you visit picture-postcard fishing villages and towns which are fabulous places to grab a pint or spend the night. In fine weather, this is a landscape that soothes the soul.

With all these delights on offer, it is surprising that the CLW is overshadowed by its more famous National Trail siblings such as the Pennine Way, the Hadrian's Wall Path and the Cotswold Way. However, perhaps this can be partially explained by nomenclature. Each of England's National Trails has a specific theme which is normally clearly referenced in that trail's name: the Pennine Way, for example, is clearly a walk across the Pennines, a chain of hills with which most people are familiar; the Cotswold Way is obviously a walk through the Cotswolds, one of England's most famous regions; and the Hadrian's Wall Path is plainly a walk along Hadrian's Wall, one of England's most important attractions. The theme of the CLW, on the other hand, is less obvious to someone who is not familiar with the Yorkshire countryside: although you might have heard of the Cleveland Hills, you could be forgiven for being unsure what the word 'Cleveland' actually refers to. In fact, Cleveland was an ancient district of Yorkshire, comprising the hills and dales between the River Tees and the Vale of Pickering: it meant 'cliff-land', referring not only to the cliffs along its coastline but also to the cliffs of the inland escarpments. However, even with this explanation, the character of the trek is not immediately apparent because there is no reference in its name to the trail's defining feature, the North York Moors. Maybe if it had a more catchy name, the CLW might find itself on the tips of more people's tongues: the 'Yorkshire Moors Way' perhaps?

The main route of the CLW is 110 miles (177km) long with approximately 13,000ft (4,000m) of ascent and descent. Those statistics may sound intimidating but it is reassuring to note that thousands of normal people complete the CLW each year: with the right preparation, planning and approach, the CLW is manageable for most people of reasonable fitness. Yes, it is a challenge but it is an achievable one. And that is where this book comes in: most of what you need to know to plan, and prepare for, the CLW is here within these pages and the entire route is described in detail to guide you on the trek itself. Furthermore, unlike some other books, this one contains real Ordnance Survey maps: for each stage, there are 1:25,000 scale maps to go with the accurate and concise route descriptions. Because all the maps are set out within the guidebook itself, there is no need to fumble about with a guidebook in one hand and a map in the other.

We aim to ensure that you have the best chance possible of completing the trek. We place great importance on the correct preparation and we focus in detail on modern lightweight equipment (see 'Equipment'). We also believe that it is crucial to match your itinerary to your experience, fitness and ability. Accordingly, we have included here an extraordinary level of detail on itinerary planning: our unique itinerary planner has 20 different itineraries to choose from. For each itinerary, we have completed for you all the difficult calculations of time, distance and altitude gain/loss. This makes it easy for you to design a manageable itinerary that suits your specific needs. Once on the trail, you will be able to relax and fully enjoy one of England's great treks.

How hard is the CLW?

Notwithstanding the challenges, thousands of hikers walk the full length of the CLW each year. It is therefore an achievable endeavour. However, each day you will need to walk a significant distance across undulating terrain so a reasonable level of fitness is required. The CLW traverses remote landscapes of hills, valleys, cliffs and moorland: you will need to climb and descend on a daily basis to negotiate the constantly undulating terrain. That said, the route has less climbing and descending than many other treks and it is considered to be one of the easiest multi-day hikes in the UK. In fact, there are only about 13,000ft (4,000m) of ascent/descent on the entire trek and these are relatively well spread out across the length of the route. Furthermore, although there are plenty of short ups and downs (which can be tiring), there are few long climbs/descents to sap your strength.

Although not absolutely necessary, previous experience of backpacking will help. If you have not previously undertaken a multi-day hike, then be aware that daily exertions take their toll on your body both physically and mentally. The fitter you are at the start of the trek, the better your chances of success and the more you will enjoy it. Accordingly, it is advisable to train in advance: there is no substitute for training hikes, carrying a pack.

Generally, the CLW uses clear paths and tracks which are simple to negotiate. There are also some short sections along minor roads. On a few occasions, you may need to climb/ descend steeply over rocks, however, you will not require any technical scrambling or climbing skills. The route is well marked and route-finding is normally straightforward using only the maps and directions provided in this book.

Most people walk the CLW in seven to ten days. However, fit and experienced hikers can finish it in six days or less and endurance runners often do it even faster. We prefer to take it easy, soaking up all the delights on offer, lingering over packed lunches whilst savouring the magnificent views, strolling through the exquisite villages and enjoying the real ale in the country pubs along the way. Usually, there is plenty of accommodation on, or near, the trail so for the most part it is simple to plan daily distances to suit your requirements.

If you plan to camp along the way then you will have to carry a lot of extra gear, unless you pay for a baggage transfer service (see page 48). This additional weight increases the difficulty of the trek and many trekkers set off carrying equipment which is unnecessary or simply too heavy: this can result in injury and/or exhaustion, leading to abandonment. For advice on lightweight gear, see p52.

Direction and start/finish points

The CLW runs between Helmsley in the W and Filey Brigg in the E. As you can hike in either direction, this book caters for both W-E and E-W trekkers: full route descriptions and plenty of different itineraries are provided for each approach. The numbered waypoints on the real maps make the route easy to follow in either direction.

Traditionally, people walk W-E and the primary reason for this approach is wind direction: the prevailing winds in the UK are from the SW or W. Accordingly, if you walk W-E, there is a higher probability that the wind will be on your back: you expend less energy walking away from the wind.

However, there are other considerations too. The first is an entirely subjective matter. The trek has two distinct phases: moor and sea. Both are spectacular but opinions vary as to which should be undertaken first and which should be left to last. In our opinion, it feels more natural to head W-E, starting with the moody, mysterious and starkly beautiful expanses of the moors and finishing with the bright and colourful Yorkshire coastline: if you can forgive the over-dramatic metaphor, it is like heading from darkness towards light which seems more positive and full of hope than moving in the other direction. Well, we told you that it was over-dramatic, didn't we?! There is absolutely nothing wrong with heading E-W and walking the coast first, if that is what you fancy.

On a more practical note, it is also worth bearing in mind that because most walkers travel W-E, that is probably the more sociable approach: you are more likely to bump into the same people each day, making it easier to develop trail friendships.

On some treks, the choice of finishing location plays an important part in determining the direction of travel: it is always lovely to finish somewhere pretty which has a variety of pubs and restaurants in which you can celebrate your success. In the case of the CLW, however, there is little to choose between Helmsley and Filey (the staging towns at either end of the trek): both are attractive and both have good places to eat and drink. That said, if we were forced to choose, Filey's seaside location would tip the balance in its favour, lending yet more support to a W-E approach to the trek.

Hiking shorter sections of the CLW

Walking the CLW in one go is a wonderful experience but there are other ways to enjoy this incredible trail. If you do not wish to walk the entire route, it is possible to walk shorter sections of it. There are numerous escape/access points along the route where you could leave or join the trek using public transport or taxis: see 'Secondary trail-heads'. You could start at any of these places and walk a few sections. Or you could skip sections by leaving the route at one of these points.

Many people prefer to hike the CLW in day-long sections using public transport to travel to/from the start and finish points: see 'Public transport along the CLW'. Over the course of months or years, they will eventually complete the entire trek. Many others have no desire to walk the CLW in its entirety and simply want to experience a few of its highlights. The Itinerary Planner should help you to plan day-walks along the CLW. Often day-walkers hike in groups, leaving a car at each end of their route.

If you only wish to walk some of the highlights of the region, then we would suggest some or all of the following options (each of which can be completed in a day):

- Sutton Bank to Osmotherley
- Osmotherley to Lordstones
- Lordstones to Kildale
- Kildale to Roseberry Topping
- Saltburn-by-the-Sea to Staithes
- Staithes to Whitby
- Whitby to Robin Hood's Bay

Guided tours, self-guided tours or independent walking?

A frequently asked question is whether to walk independently or with an organised group. The answer is a personal one and depends upon your own particular circumstances and requirements. For many, the decision to organise the trek themselves, and to walk independently, can be almost life-changing, opening the door for other challenges in the future. There is much satisfaction to be gained from planning and navigating a trek yourself and the sense of achievement on completion is to be savoured.

However, the independent trekker usually carries a full pack and is responsible for all daily decisions such as pacing, which way to go at junctions, when to stock up with food and water, and choice of route in bad weather. For some, this will be too great a burden on top of the physical effort required simply to walk the route. For those walkers, a guided group is a great solution: the tour company typically organises food, accommodation and transfer of luggage each night. And the guide makes all the decisions, enabling the walker to concentrate on the walking. There are a few tour companies operating guided trips on the CLW but you should check whether they cover the full official route or just some of the highlights.

Self-guided tours are much more popular and are a sensible middle-ground. The tour company books all the accommodation and provides advice and information on walking the route. However, you will walk the trail without a guide. Normally, your breakfast will be provided and you can request packed lunches. For evening meals, they will usually provide details of pubs and restaurants which are within walking distance of your accommodation. Often, they can transfer your baggage to your accommodation each night so you only need to carry a small day-pack on the trail. As an alternative, there are also a few businesses offering baggage transfer services to independent trekkers: see p48.

In fact, with the rise in the number of businesses offering self-guided tours and the recent decline in the number of B&Bs, some of the accommodation along the CLW is block-booked months in advance by the tour companies. At peak times, this makes it harder for the independent trekker to secure first-choice accommodation unless booked well in advance. As a result, many confident trekkers (who would be perfectly capable of walking independently) book a self-guided trip simply to avail of the accommodation booking service. By booking a self-guided tour or using an accommodation booking service, much of the hassle of planning the trek is alleviated, albeit at a price.

When to go

The main trekking season runs from Easter to October. Before Easter and after October, some accommodation will be closed. The weather in Britain is notoriously wet and in Northern England, the rain is legendary. Accordingly, you should prepare for some wet weather on the CLW, irrespective of the season. That is not to say that it always rains: it is just that statistics dictate that there is a good chance that this will happen at some point along your trek. That said, some seasons are statistically drier than others and you can maximise your chances of good weather by selecting a drier month.

However, weather is not the only consideration: Yorkshire is busier in high summer, making the trails busier and accommodation more difficult to find. Campers will also be interested to know that the pesky midge makes an appearance in June, July and August: although they are not as pervasive as in Scotland, their presence can be quite annoying in the evenings and early mornings. The relative merits of each season are discussed in detail below.

Spring (March to May): this can be the most beautiful time of year for walking. Many wild-flowers are on show and the gorse will also be in full bloom with its vivid yellow flowers and coconut aroma. By May, new growth will be upon the deciduous plants and grass is at its greenest. The weather is often sunny and warm and May can be the finest month in England. Of course, rain is a possibility in spring but it usually becomes drier as the season progresses. Visibility in spring is generally excellent so views are wide-ranging. Early in spring, the number of walkers is lower (except at Easter), gradually increasing throughout the season. Normally, the midges only start to make an appearance at the end of May.

Summer (June to August): this is the peak walking season and visitor numbers are at their greatest. The trails are busy and accommodation is harder to find. The days are long and statistically, your chances of good weather are highest in this period. In recent years, the weather in June has tended to be more settled than in July and August. Temperatures are at their peak and there is sometimes haze. There are still plenty of flowers on show throughout the summer and towards the end of the period, the heather comes into bloom painting the moors a magnificent purple colour: August is usually the best month for the heather bloom. This is the worst period for midges.

Autumn (September to November): although visitor numbers reduce, September is still a busy month on the CLW. As soon as children return to school, retired folk and those without kids come out to play. Autumn often provides excellent walking conditions. The weather in September/October can be more settled, with less rain, than in summer:

temperatures are lower but still comfortable. Skies can be very clear giving excellent visibility and the quality of the low light is magnificent. The wide variety of deciduous plants in the UK means that the autumn colours are stunning. However, as the days get shorter, it is wise to start walking early: if something were to go wrong, you would have less daylight in which to seek help than in summer. By September, the midges are on the decline and the situation improves throughout the autumn. The weather in November tends to be less conducive to pleasant walking and some accommodation will be closed.

Winter (December to February): these are the coldest months and rain is more likely. Occasionally, there is snow which can be a delight for a suitably-equipped walker, although care should be taken. Navigation on the moors can be tricky in snowy conditions and accordingly, this is best left to those with the appropriate winter experience and the correct equipment. Even if there is no snow, watch out for ice which forms in places where water collects. Cold months sometimes bring crisp, clear weather and the low sun makes the light very beautiful. A sunny day in winter can be one of the best of the year. Days are short so start early. Much accommodation will be closed. A winter assault on the CLW is for hardy hikers only.

Season	Pros	Cons
Spring	Pleasant temperatures Frequent sunny skies Good visibility Gorse and wild-flowers Fewer visitors Normally midge-free	Rainy spells are common in March and April Ground can be wet
Summer	Best chance of fine weather Ground is often dry Heather blooms	Sometimes hazy August sometimes wet Visitor numbers highest Midges are most active
Autumn	Pleasant temperatures Frequent sunny skies Excellent visibility Fewer visitors Normally midge-free Autumn colours	Shorter days Cooler evenings Rainy spells
Winter	Sometimes crisp clear skies Excellent visibility Fewer visitors No midges	Shortest days Can be cold and icy Rainy spells Occasionally, there is snow

Beach huts in Scarborough (Stage 9d/10a)

Using this book

This book is designed to be used by walkers of differing abilities. Many guidebooks for long-distance treks rigidly divide the route into a fixed number of long day-stages, leaving it up to walkers themselves to break down those stages to design daily routes which suit their abilities. This book, however, has been laid out differently to give the trekker flexibility: it divides the route into 28 shorter stages which you can combine to design daily routes that meet your own specific needs.

Each of the 28 stages covers the distance between one accommodation option and the subsequent one. Most accommodation options on the route are the start/finish point of a stage. You can choose how many of these stages you wish to walk each day. Each stage has its own walk description, route map and elevation profile.

The labelling of the stages uses a combination of numbers and letters. It is a simple system but requires a little bit of explanation. Firstly, we have divided the route into 10 'Sections' (numbered from 1 to 10 from W-E): each Section represents one day of our standard 10-day schedule. Within each Section, the route is broken down into stages: every stage is labelled with a number between 1 and 10, representing the relevant Section that the stage is part of. Every stage is also labelled with a letter. So, for example, the first stage in Section 2 is 'Stage 2a', the next stage is 'Stage 2b' and so on. Take a look at the detailed Itinerary Planner below and all should become clear.

The Itinerary Planner includes a range of tables outlining 20 suggested itineraries of 5, 6, 7, 8, 9, 10 and 11 days. We include itineraries for both W-E and E-W trekkers. In each table, the maths have been done for you so there is no need for you to waste time (and mental strength) working out daily distances, timings and altitude gain.

Of course, the suggested itineraries are only suggestions. You can shorten or lengthen your day in any number of ways to suit yourself: just decide how many stages you want to walk that day. It is up to you. As there is accommodation at the end of most stages, it is easy to design your own bespoke itinerary and adjust it on the ground as you go along (subject to availability of accommodation).

For example, day 9 of the standard 10-day route involves walking Stages 9a, 9b, 9c and 9d. However, you could decide to extend your day by walking Stages 9a, 9b, 9c, 9d and 10a, all on the same day. Or you might be tired and decide to shorten your day by walking only Stages 9a, 9b and 9c. With some other guidebooks, you would have to work out how to split stages yourself, involving some complicated maths to plan distances and times going forward. This guide, however, does all the hard mental work for you.

In this book:

Timings indicate the approximate time required by a reasonably fit walker to complete a stage. They do not include stoppage time. Do not get frustrated if your own times do not match ours: everyone walks at different speeds. As you progress through the trek, you will soon learn how your own times compare with those given here and you will adjust your plans accordingly.

Walking distances are given in both miles and kilometres (km). One mile equates to approximately 1.6km.

Place names in brackets in the route descriptions indicate the direction to be followed on signposts. For example, "('Whitby')" would mean that you follow a sign for Whitby.

Ascent/descent numbers are the aggregate of all the altitude gain or loss (measured in feet/metres) on the uphill or downhill sections of a stage. As a rule of thumb, a fit walker climbs 1000 to 1300 feet (300 to 400m) in an hour. The statistics tables in the route descriptions are based on W-E itineraries: E-W trekkers should simply swap the ascent and descent figures.

Elevation profiles are provided for each Section, indicating where the climbs and descents fall on the route. The profiles are based on W-E itineraries: E-W walkers should simply read them in reverse.

Spellings of place names are normally derived from the OS maps. However, there is sometimes disagreement over how places are spelt. Accordingly, you may notice different spellings elsewhere.

Real maps are provided. These are extracts from 1:25,000 scale Explorer maps produced by OS, the mapping agency for GB. The maps are divided into 4cm grid squares: each square represents 1km x 1km. On the maps, we have marked the route of the trek, the start/finish points of stages, significant waypoints and the accommodation on the CLW. On each map, N is at the top of the page.

The following abbreviations are used:

BCE	Before the Common Era (a secular alternative to 'BC')
CE	The Common Era (a secular alternative to 'AD')
CLW	The Cleveland Way
GB	Great Britain
NYMNP	North York Moors National Park
OR	Off-route
OS	Ordnance Survey
RHB	Robin Hood's Bay
WW1/WW2	World War 1/World War 2
TL	Turn left
TR	Turn right
SH	Straight ahead
N, S, E and W, etc.	North, South, East and West, etc.
W-E	West to East
E-W	East to West

The path along Hunt Cliff (Stage 6a)

Itinerary Planner: West to East

Stage	Start	Time (hr)	Distance		Ascent		Descent	
			miles	km	ft	m	ft	m
1a	Helmsley	1:45	3.5	5.7	436	133	256	78
1b	Scawton exit	2:00	4.1	6.6	686	209	92	28
1c	Sutton Bank Junction	0:30	1.3	2.1	13	4	213	65
2a	Kilburn exit	2:00	4.5	7.3	397	121	180	55
2b	Boltby exit	0:45	1.4	2.3	207	63	144	44
2c	High Paradise Farm	3:15	7.3	11.7	489	149	1014	309
3a	Osmotherley	4:00	7.8	12.5	1647	502	1211	369
3b	Lordstones	0:45	1.5	2.4	476	145	394	120
4	Great Broughton exit	5:45	11.3	18.2	1476	450	1962	598
5a	Kildale	2:15	4.5	7.2	1073	327	581	177
5b	Roseberry Topping (Newton-under-Roseberry exit)	2:45	6.0	9.6	666	203	1322	403
5c	Slapewath	1:00	2.2	3.5	331	101	223	68
5d	Skelton Green	0:15	0.4	0.6	0	0	157	48
5e	Skelton	1:00	2.2	3.5	141	43	351	107
6a	Saltburn-by-the-Sea	1:45	4.0	6.5	308	94	436	133
6b	Skinningrove	2:30	5.1	8.2	696	212	696	212
7a	Staithes	1:00	1.9	3.0	335	102	33	10
7b	Port Mulgrave	0:30	1.6	2.6	92	28	144	44
7c	Runswick Bank Top	1:45	3.9	6.2	482	147	440	134
7d	Lythe exit	0:30	1.5	2.4	23	7	289	88
7e	Sandsend	1:30	3.4	5.5	210	64	220	67
8	Whitby	3:30	7.3	11.8	702	214	722	220
9a	Robin Hood's Bay	0:15	0.7	1.1	135	41	98	30
9b	Boggle Hole	1:30	2.9	4.6	692	211	125	38
9c	Ravenscar	1:30	4.1	6.6	125	38	650	198
9d	Hayburn Wyke	3:30	7.8	12.5	427	130	502	153
10a	Scarborough	1:45	3.9	6.3	472	144	348	106
10b	Cayton exit	1:45	4.5	7.2	246	75	240	73
Finish	Filey Brigg							

Itinerary Planner: East to West

Stage	Start	Time (hr)	Distance		Ascent		Descent	
			miles	km	ft	m	ft	m
10b	Filey Brigg	1:45	4.5	7.2	240	73	246	75
10a	Cayton exit	1:45	3.9	6.3	348	106	472	144
9d	Scarborough	3:30	7.8	12.5	502	153	427	130
9c	Hayburn Wyke	1:45	4.1	6.6	650	198	125	38
9b	Ravenscar	1:15	2.9	4.6	125	38	692	211
9a	Boggle Hole	0:15	0.7	1.1	98	30	135	41
8	Robin Hood's Bay	3:30	7.3	11.8	722	220	702	214
7e	Whitby	1:30	3.4	5.5	220	67	210	64
7d	Sandsend	0:45	1.5	2.4	289	88	23	7
7c	Lythe exit	1:45	3.9	6.2	440	134	482	147
7b	Runswick Bank Top	0:30	1.6	2.6	144	44	92	28
7a	Port Mulgrave	0:45	1.9	3.0	33	10	335	102
6b	Staithes	2:30	5.1	8.2	696	212	696	212
6a	Skinningrove	1:45	4.0	6.5	436	133	308	94
5e	Saltburn-by-the-Sea	1:00	2.2	3.5	351	107	141	43
5d	Skelton	0:15	0.4	0.6	157	48	0	0
5c	Skelton Green	1:00	2.2	3.5	223	68	331	101
5b	Slapewath	3:15	6.0	9.6	1322	403	666	203
5a	Roseberry Topping (Newton-under-Roseberry exit)	2:00	4.5	7.2	581	177	1073	327
4	Kildale	6:00	11.3	18.2	1962	598	1476	450
3b	Great Broughton exit	0:45	1.5	2.4	394	120	476	145
3a	Lordstones	3:45	7.8	12.5	1211	369	1647	502
2c	Osmotherley	3:30	7.3	11.7	1014	309	489	149
2b	High Paradise Farm	0:45	1.4	2.3	144	44	207	63
2a	Boltby exit	1:45	4.5	7.3	180	55	397	121
1c	Kilburn exit	0:30	1.3	2.1	213	65	13	4
1b	Sutton Bank Junction	1:45	4.1	6.6	92	28	686	209
1a	Skawton exit	1:45	3.5	5.7	256	78	436	133
Finish	Helmsley							

Suggested Itineraries: West to East

11 Days (W-E): similar to the standard 10 day Option A itinerary except that Section 5 (between Kildale and Saltburn) is spread out over two days with a night at Slapewath. Although day 6 is short, you will have plenty of time to spend in lovely Saltburn.

Day	Stages	Time (hr)	Distance		Ascent		Descent	
			miles	km	ft	m	ft	m
1	1a, 1b, 1c	4:15	8.9	14.4	1135	346	561	171
2	2a, 2b, 2c	6:00	13.2	21.3	1093	333	1339	408
3	3a, 3b	4:45	9.3	14.9	2123	647	1604	489
4	4	5:45	11.3	18.2	1476	450	1962	598
5	5a, 5b	5:00	10.4	16.8	1739	530	1903	580
6	5c, 5d, 5e	2:15	4.7	7.6	472	144	732	223
7	6a, 6b	4:15	9.1	14.7	1004	306	1132	345
8	7a, 7b, 7c, 7d, 7e	5:15	12.2	19.7	1142	348	1125	343
9	8	3:30	7.3	11.8	702	214	722	220
10	9a, 9b, 9c	3:15	7.6	12.3	951	290	873	266
11	9d, 10a, 10b	7:00	16.2	26.0	1145	349	1089	332

10 Days Option A (W-E): our standard schedule which is popular with many walkers because the nightly stops are at some of the loveliest places on the CLW (usually with a pub or two and good places to stay). These include Osmotherley, Saltburn, Staithes, Whitby and RHB. However, because it focuses on overnight stops, it is not the most balanced itinerary. Days 5 and 9 are long.

Day	Stages	Time (hr)	Distance		Ascent		Descent	
			miles	km	ft	m	ft	m
1	1a, 1b, 1c	4:15	8.9	14.4	1135	346	561	171
2	2a, 2b, 2c	6:00	13.2	21.3	1093	333	1339	408
3	3a, 3b	4:45	9.3	14.9	2123	647	1604	489
4	4	5:45	11.3	18.2	1476	450	1962	598
5	5a, 5b, 5c, 5d, 5e	7:15	15.2	24.4	2211	674	2635	803
6	6a, 6b	4:15	9.1	14.7	1004	306	1132	345
7	7a, 7b, 7c, 7d, 7e	5:15	12.2	19.7	1142	348	1125	343
8	8	3:30	7.3	11.8	702	214	722	220
9	9a, 9b, 9c, 9d	6:45	15.4	24.8	1378	420	1375	419
10	10a, 10b	3:30	8.4	13.5	719	219	587	179

10 Days Option B (W-E): identical to 10 day Option A except that it avoids an overnight stay in Scarborough. The hotel at Hayburn Wyke is a peaceful alternative.

Day	Stages	Time (hr)	Distance		Ascent		Descent	
			miles	km	ft	m	ft	m
1	1a, 1b, 1c	4:15	8.9	14.4	1135	346	561	171
2	2a, 2b, 2c	6:00	13.2	21.3	1093	333	1339	408
3	3a, 3b	4:45	9.3	14.9	2123	647	1604	489
4	4	5:45	11.3	18.2	1476	450	1962	598
5	5a, 5b, 5c, 5d, 5e	7:15	15.2	24.4	2211	674	2635	803
6	6a, 6b	4:15	9.1	14.7	1004	306	1132	345
7	7a, 7b, 7c, 7d, 7e	5:15	12.2	19.7	1142	348	1125	343
8	8	3:30	7.3	11.8	702	214	722	220
9	9a, 9b, 9c	3:15	7.6	12.3	951	290	873	266
10	9d, 10a, 10b	7:00	16.2	26.0	1145	349	1089	332

10 Days Option C (W-E): identical to 10 day Option B except that you stay at the hotel at Slapewath instead of Saltburn. It also avoids the need for an overnight stay in Scarborough: the hotel at Hayburn Wyke is a more peaceful alternative.

Day	Stages	Time (hr)	Distance		Ascent		Descent	
			miles	km	ft	m	ft	m
1	1a, 1b, 1c	4:15	8.9	14.4	1135	346	561	171
2	2a, 2b, 2c	6:00	13.2	21.3	1093	333	1339	408
3	3a, 3b	4:45	9.3	14.9	2123	647	1604	489
4	4	5:45	11.3	18.2	1476	450	1962	598
5	5a, 5b	5:00	10.4	16.8	1739	530	1903	580
6	5c, 5d, 5e, 6a, 6b	6:30	13.9	22.3	1476	450	1864	568
7	7a, 7b, 7c, 7d, 7e	5:15	12.2	19.7	1142	348	1125	343
8	8	3:30	7.3	11.8	702	214	722	220
9	9a, 9b, 9c	3:15	7.6	12.3	951	290	873	266
10	9d, 10a, 10b	7:00	16.2	26.0	1145	349	1089	332

9 Days Option A (W-E): similar to the standard 10 day Option A itinerary except that Sections 8 to 10 (between Whitby and Filey Brigg) are walked in two days instead of three. This avoids the need for an overnight stay in Scarborough (which is not to everyone's taste). Although you will not spend the night at the lovely RHB, the hotel at Hayburn Wyke is a peaceful alternative.

Day	Stages	Time (hr)	Distance		Ascent		Descent	
			miles	km	ft	m	ft	m
1	1a, 1b, 1c	4:15	8.9	14.4	1135	346	561	171
2	2a, 2b, 2c	6:00	13.2	21.3	1093	333	1339	408
3	3a, 3b	4:45	9.3	14.9	2123	647	1604	489
4	4	5:45	11.3	18.2	1476	450	1962	598
5	5a, 5b, 5c, 5d, 5e	7:15	15.2	24.4	2211	674	2635	803
6	6a, 6b	4:15	9.1	14.7	1004	306	1132	345
7	7a, 7b, 7c, 7d, 7e	5:15	12.2	19.7	1142	348	1125	343
8	8, 9a, 9b, 9c	6:45	15.0	24.1	1654	504	1595	486
9	9d, 10a, 10b	7:00	16.2	26.0	1145	349	1089	332

9 Days Option B (W-E): similar to the standard 10 day Option A itinerary except that Sections 6 to 8 (between Saltburn and RHB) are walked in two days instead of three. You will overnight in the wonderful RHB but unfortunately, you will not stay in Staithes or Whitby. Furthermore, you will also stop for the night in Scarborough (which is not to everyone's taste).

Day	Stages	Time (hr)	Distance		Ascent		Descent	
			miles	km	ft	m	ft	m
1	1a, 1b, 1c	4:15	8.9	14.4	1135	346	561	171
2	2a, 2b, 2c	6:00	13.2	21.3	1093	333	1339	408
3	3a, 3b	4:45	9.3	14.9	2123	647	1604	489
4	4	5:45	11.3	18.2	1476	450	1962	598
5	5a, 5b, 5c, 5d, 5e	7:15	15.2	24.4	2211	674	2635	803
6	6a, 6b, 7a, 7b	5:45	12.6	20.3	1431	436	1309	399
7	7c, 7d, 7e, 8	7:15	16.1	25.9	1417	432	1670	509
8	9a, 9b, 9c, 9d	6:45	15.4	24.8	1378	420	1375	419
9	10a, 10b	3:30	8.4	13.5	719	219	587	179

8 Days (W-E): similar to 9 Day Option A except that Sections 1 to 3 (between Helmsley and Great Broughton) are walked in two days instead of three. This makes for a tough start to the trek. Although, you will not stop overnight in Osmotherley, a night at High Paradise Farm should be adequate compensation.

Day	Stages	Time (hr)	Distance		Ascent		Descent	
			miles	km	ft	m	ft	m
1	1a, 1b, 1c, 2a, 2b	7:00	14.9	24.0	1739	530	886	270
2	2c, 3a, 3b	8:00	16.5	26.6	2612	796	2618	798
3	4	5:45	11.3	18.2	1476	450	1962	598
4	5a, 5b, 5c, 5d, 5e	7:15	15.2	24.4	2211	674	2635	803
5	6a, 6b	4:15	9.1	14.7	1004	306	1132	345
6	7a, 7b, 7c, 7d, 7e	5:15	12.2	19.7	1142	348	1125	343
7	8, 9a, 9b, 9c	6:45	15.0	24.1	1654	504	1595	486
8	9d, 10a, 10b	7:00	16.2	26.0	1145	349	1089	332

7 Days (W-E): similar to the 8 Day itinerary except that Sections 4 to 6 (between Great Broughton and Staithes) are walked in two days instead of three. Days 2, 3 and 4 are long and tiring

Day	Stages	Time (hr)	Distance		Ascent		Descent	
			miles	km	ft	m	ft	m
1	1a, 1b, 1c, 2a, 2b	7:00	14.9	24.0	1739	530	886	270
2	2c, 3a, 3b	8:00	16.5	26.6	2612	796	2618	798
3	4, 5a	8:00	15.8	25.4	2549	777	2543	775
4	5b, 5c, 5d, 5e, 6a, 6b	9:15	19.8	31.9	2142	653	3186	971
5	7a, 7b, 7c, 7d, 7e	5:15	12.2	19.7	1142	348	1125	343
6	8, 9a, 9b, 9c	6:45	15.0	24.1	1654	504	1595	486
7	9d, 10a, 10b	7:00	16.2	26.0	1145	349	1089	332

6 Days (W-E): for fit hikers. Every day is long and hard

Day	Stages	Time (hr)	Distance		Ascent		Descent	
			miles	km	ft	m	ft	m
1	1a, 1b, 1c, 2a, 2b	7:00	14.9	24.0	1739	530	886	270
2	2c, 3a, 3b	8:00	16.5	26.6	2612	796	2618	798
3	4, 5a, 5b	10:45	21.8	35.0	3215	980	3865	1178
4	5c, 5d, 5e, 6a, 6b, 7a, 7b	8:00	17.3	27.9	1903	580	2041	622
5	7c, 7d, 7e, 8, 9a, 9b	9:00	19.6	31.6	2244	684	1893	577
6	9c, 9d, 10a, 10b	8:30	20.3	32.6	1270	387	1739	530

5 Days (W-E): for fit hikers and runners only. Every day is long and hard

Day	Stages	Time (hr)	Distance		Ascent		Descent	
			miles	km	ft	m	ft	m
1	1a, 1b, 1c, 2a, 2b, 2c	10:15	22.2	35.7	2228	679	1900	579
2	3a, 3b, 4	10:30	20.6	33.1	3599	1097	3566	1087
3	5a, 5b, 5c, 5d, 5e, 6a, 6b	11:30	24.3	39.1	3215	980	3767	1148
4	7a, 7b, 7c, 7d, 7e, 8	8:45	19.6	31.5	1844	562	1847	563
5	9a, 9b, 9c, 9d, 10a, 10b	10:15	23.8	38.3	2097	639	1962	598

Suggested Itineraries: East to West

11 Days (E-W): similar to the standard 10 day Option A itinerary except that Section 5 (between Saltburn and Kildale) is spread out over two days with a night at Slapewath. Day 6 is short but you could spend the morning relaxing in the seaside town of Saltburn.

Day	Stages	Time (hr)	Distance		Ascent		Descent	
			miles	km	ft	m	ft	m
1	10b, 10a	3:30	8.4	13.5	588	179	718	219
2	9d, 9c, 9b, 9a	6:45	15.4	24.8	1375	419	1378	420
3	8	3:30	7.3	11.8	722	220	702	214
4	7e, 7d, 7c, 7b, 7a	5:15	12.2	19.7	1125	343	1142	348
5	6b, 6a	4:15	9.1	14.7	1132	345	1004	306
6	5e, 5d, 5c	2:15	4.7	7.6	732	223	472	144
7	5b, 5a	5:15	10.4	16.8	1903	580	1739	530
8	4	6:00	11.3	18.2	1962	598	1476	450
9	3b, 3a	4:30	9.3	14.9	1604	489	2123	647
10	2c, 2b, 2a	6:00	13.2	21.3	1339	408	1093	333
11	1c, 1b, 1a	4:00	8.9	14.4	561	171	1135	346

10 Days Option A (E-W): Our standard schedule which is popular with many walkers because the nightly stops are at some of the loveliest places on the CLW (usually with a pub or two and good places to stay). These include Osmotherley, Saltburn, Staithes Whitby and RHB. However, because it focuses on overnight stops, it is not the most balanced itinerary. Days 2 and 6 are long.

Day	Stages	Time (hr)	Distance		Ascent		Descent	
			miles	km	ft	m	ft	m
1	10b, 10a	3:30	8.4	13.5	588	179	718	219
2	9d, 9c, 9b, 9a	6:45	15.4	24.8	1375	419	1378	420
3	8	3:30	7.3	11.8	722	220	702	214
4	7e, 7d, 7c, 7b, 7a	5:15	12.2	19.7	1125	343	1142	348
5	6b, 6a	4:15	9.1	14.7	1132	345	1004	306
6	5e, 5d, 5c, 5b, 5a	7:30	15.2	24.4	2635	803	2211	674
7	4	6:00	11.3	18.2	1962	598	1476	450
8	3b, 3a	4:30	9.3	14.9	1604	489	2123	647
9	2c, 2b, 2a	6:00	13.2	21.3	1339	408	1093	333
10	1c, 1b, 1a	4:00	8.9	14.4	561	171	1135	346

10 Days Option B (E-W): identical to 10 day Option A except that it avoids an overnight stay in Scarborough. The long first day is a tough start to the CLW.

Day	Stages	Time (hr)	Distance		Ascent		Descent	
			miles	km	ft	m	ft	m
1	10b, 10a, 9d	7:00	16.2	26.0	1090	332	1145	349
2	9c, 9b, 9a	3:15	7.6	12.3	873	266	951	290
3	8	3:30	7.3	11.8	722	220	702	214
4	7e, 7d, 7c, 7b, 7a	5:15	12.2	19.7	1125	343	1142	348
5	6b, 6a	4:15	9.1	14.7	1132	345	1004	306
6	5e, 5d, 5c, 5b, 5a	7:30	15.2	24.4	2635	803	2211	674
7	4	6:00	11.3	18.2	1962	598	1476	450
8	3b, 3a	4:30	9.3	14.9	1604	489	2123	647
9	2c, 2b, 2a	6:00	13.2	21.3	1339	408	1093	333
10	1c, 1b, 1a	4:00	8.9	14.4	561	171	1135	346

10 Days Option C (E-W): identical to 10 day Option B except that you stay at the hotel at Slapewath instead of Saltburn. It also avoids the need for an overnight stay in Scarborough. The hotel at Hayburn Wyke is a more peaceful alternative. The long first day is a tough start to the CLW.

Day	Stages	Time (hr)	Distance		Ascent		Descent	
			miles	km	ft	m	ft	m
1	10b, 10a, 9d	7:00	16.2	26.0	1090	332	1145	349
2	9c, 9b, 9a	3:15	7.6	12.3	873	266	951	290
3	8	3:30	7.3	11.8	722	220	702	214
4	7e, 7d, 7c, 7b, 7a	5:15	12.2	19.7	1125	343	1142	348
5	6b, 6a, 5e, 5d, 5c	6:30	13.9	22.3	1864	568	1476	450
6	5b, 5a	5:15	10.4	16.8	1903	580	1739	530
7	4	6:00	11.3	18.2	1962	598	1476	450
8	3b, 3a	4:30	9.3	14.9	1604	489	2123	647
9	2c, 2b, 2a	6:00	13.2	21.3	1339	408	1093	333
10	1c, 1b, 1a	4:00	8.9	14.4	561	171	1135	346

9 Days Option A (E-W): similar to the standard 10 day Option A itinerary except that Sections 8 to 6 (between RHB and Saltburn) are walked in two days instead of three. You will overnight in the wonderful RHB but unfortunately, you will not stay in Staithes or Whitby. Furthermore, you will also stop for the night in Scarborough (which is not to everyone's taste).

Day	Stages	Time (hr)	Distance		Ascent		Descent	
			miles	km	ft	m	ft	m
1	10b, 10a	3:30	8.4	13.5	588	179	718	219
2	9d, 9c, 9b, 9a	6:45	15.4	24.8	1375	419	1378	420
3	8, 7e, 7d, 7c	7:30	16.1	25.9	1670	509	1417	432
4	7b, 7a, 6b, 6a	5:30	12.6	20.3	1309	399	1431	436
5	5e, 5d, 5c, 5b, 5a	7:30	15.2	24.4	2635	803	2211	674
6	4	6:00	11.3	18.2	1962	598	1476	450
7	3b, 3a	4:30	9.3	14.9	1604	489	2123	647
8	2c, 2b, 2a	6:00	13.2	21.3	1339	408	1093	333
9	1c, 1b, 1a	4:00	8.9	14.4	561	171	1135	346

9 Days Option B (E-W): similar to the standard 10 day Option A itinerary except that Sections 10 to 8 (between Filey Brigg and Whitby) are walked in two days instead of three. This avoids the need for an overnight stay in Scarborough. Although you will not spend the night at the lovely RHB, the hotel at Hayburn Wyke is a peaceful alternative.

Day	Stages	Time (hr)	Distance		Ascent		Descent	
			miles	km	ft	m	ft	m
1	10b, 10a, 9d	7:00	16.2	26.0	1090	332	1145	349
2	9c, 9b, 9a, 8	6:45	15.0	24.1	1595	486	1654	504
3	7e, 7d, 7c, 7b, 7a	5:15	12.2	19.7	1125	343	1142	348
4	6b, 6a	4:15	9.1	14.7	1132	345	1004	306
5	5e, 5d, 5c, 5b, 5a	7:30	15.2	24.4	2635	803	2211	674
6	4	6:00	11.3	18.2	1962	598	1476	450
7	3b, 3a	4:30	9.3	14.9	1604	489	2123	647
8	2c, 2b, 2a	6:00	13.2	21.3	1339	408	1093	333
9	1c, 1b, 1a	4:00	8.9	14.4	561	171	1135	346

8 Days (E-W): similar to 9 Day Option B except that Sections 3 to 1 (between Great Broughton and Helmsley) are walked in two days instead of three. Day 7 is very tough. Although, you will not stop overnight in Osmotherley, a night at High Paradise Farm should be adequate compensation.

Day	Stages	Time (hr)	Distance		Ascent		Descent	
			miles	km	ft	m	ft	m
1	10b, 10a, 9d	7:00	16.2	26.0	1090	332	1145	349
2	9c, 9b, 9a, 8	6:45	15.0	24.1	1595	486	1654	504
3	7e, 7d, 7c, 7b, 7a	5:15	12.2	19.7	1125	343	1142	348
4	6b, 6a	4:15	9.1	14.7	1132	345	1004	306
5	5e, 5d, 5c, 5b, 5a	7:30	15.2	24.4	2635	803	2211	674
6	4	6:00	11.3	18.2	1962	598	1476	450
7	3b, 3a, 2c	8:00	16.5	26.6	2618	798	2612	796
8	2b, 2a, 1c, 1b, 1a	6:30	14.9	24.0	886	270	1739	530

7 Days (E-W): similar to the 8 Day itinerary except that Sections 6 to 4 (between Staithes and Great Broughton) are walked in two days instead of three. Days 4, 5 and 6 are long and tiring.

Day	Stages	Time (hr)	Distance		Ascent		Descent	
			miles	km	ft	m	ft	m
1	10b, 10a, 9d	7:00	16.2	26.0	1090	332	1145	349
2	9c, 9b, 9a, 8	6:45	15.0	24.1	1595	486	1654	504
3	7e, 7d, 7c, 7b, 7a	5:15	12.2	19.7	1125	343	1142	348
4	6b, 6a, 5e, 5d, 5c, 5b	9:45	19.8	31.9	3186	971	2142	653
5	5a, 4	8:00	15.8	25.4	2543	775	2549	777
6	3b, 3a, 2c	8:00	16.5	26.6	2618	798	2612	796
7	2b, 2a, 1c, 1b, 1a	6:30	14.9	24.0	886	270	1739	530

6 Days (E-W): for fit hikers. Every day is long but day 4 is particularly difficult.

Day	Stages	Time (hr)	Distance		Ascent		Descent	
			miles	km	ft	m	ft	m
1	10b, 10a, 9d, 9c	8:45	20.3	32.6	1740	530	1269	387
2	9b, 9a, 8, 7e, 7d, 7c	9:00	19.6	31.6	1893	577	2244	684
3	7b, 7a, 6b, 6a, 5e, 5d, 5c	7:45	17.3	27.9	2041	622	1903	580
4	5b, 5a, 4	11:15	21.8	35.0	3865	1178	3215	980
5	3b, 3a, 2c	8:00	16.5	26.6	2618	798	2612	796
6	2b, 2a, 1c, 1b, 1a	6:30	14.9	24.0	886	270	1739	530

5 Days (E-W): for fit hikers and runners only. Every day is long and hard.

Day	Stages	Time (hr)	Distance		Ascent		Descent	
			miles	km	ft	m	ft	m
1	10b, 10a, 9d, 9c, 9b, 9a	10:15	23.8	38.3	1963	598	2096	639
2	8, 7e, 7d, 7c, 7b, 7a	8:45	19.6	31.5	1847	563	1844	562
3	6b, 6a, 5e, 5d, 5c, 5b, 5a	11:45	24.3	39.1	3767	1148	3215	980
4	4, 3b, 3a	10:30	20.6	33.1	3566	1087	3599	1097
5	2c, 2b, 2a, 1c, 1b, 1a	10:00	22.2	35.7	1900	579	2228	679

Accommodation

Osmotherley (Stage 2c/3a)

The CLW is a popular trek and there is a wide range of accommodation: 'bed and breakfasts', pubs, hotels, hostels and bunkhouses/camping barns. All accommodation is numbered and marked on the OS maps in this book. Detailed accommodation listings are provided on pages 23 to 31. All contact details were correct at the date of press but this information frequently changes: since Covid, pubs and B&Bs have been closing down in the UK at an alarming rate and others have been converted into self-catering holiday accommodation (usually requiring stays of at least 2 nights). Please let us know about any changes you notice.

You can often find additional accommodation options at www.airbnb.co.uk: these are normally apartments, cottages or rooms in private houses that are let to tourists. The Airbnb accommodation on offer changes so regularly that information quickly becomes outdated: consequently, we are not able to include it in our listings.

For camping, see page 21.

In many places, there is accommodation close to the trail itself. However, in some locations (particularly, on the inland half of the route), you may have to walk a mile or two away from the trail to find somewhere to stay. Accommodation along the trail tends to book up very quickly. As you move further away from the trail, bookings are often easier to secure. In the accommodation listings, any off-route accommodation is labelled 'OR' and we specify its distance from the trail. Bear in mind that the extra time and distance required to travel to, and from, OR accommodation is excluded from the statistics for each stage in the Itinerary Planner: if you intend to stay OR, you will need to allow for this extra time and effort when planning. Some OR B&Bs may be willing to pick you up from the trail and leave you back the next morning: check when booking. Alternatively, there are local taxi businesses which can pick you up: see 'Public transport along the CLW'.

These days, most people book the accommodation for their entire trip before they depart. The rise in the number of companies offering unguided trips and the decrease in the number of B&Bs mean that an increasing number of beds are block-booked months in advance by tour companies. This makes it harder for the independent trekker to secure some of the best locations unless you book well in advance or you are prepared to camp.

In July/August and during other public holidays, the trail is very busy and forward booking is normally essential. You might get lucky and be able to cobble together a set of bookings at the last minute but you are unlikely to get 'first-choice' accommodation right next to the trail.

Even outside of July/August, it is wise to book ahead, particularly at weekends and on stages where there is only one place to stay. That said, in April, May, June, September and October, it is still possible for the independent trekker to secure last-minute bookings, particularly if you are flexible with dates and places and are prepared to stay in towns/villages which are a short distance OR. Sadly though, with each year that passes, this becomes more difficult.

In April (excluding Easter) and October, fewer people walk the route so there is less demand for accommodation. Before April, and from November onwards, some accommodation may be closed so check in advance. For more booking tips, see page 31.

Bed & Breakfasts (B&Bs): traditionally, these were private homes which offered rooms and breakfast to visitors. Nowadays, however, you find many bigger and more professionally run properties. Bed and breakfast normally cost £35-75 per person sharing a double/twin room. Rates for solo travellers are usually higher because they pay a single occupancy rate. Normally, the ensuite bedrooms are basic but clean and comfortable. 'Full English' breakfast is the norm: a large helping of bacon, sausage, eggs, mushrooms and black pudding. Most do not provide evening meals but the owner should be able to recommend a local pub or restaurant. Most B&Bs have their own websites and many list their rooms on the generic travel booking sites such as expedia.com or booking.com.

Pubs & Inns: most villages have a pub and many of them offer bed and breakfast accommodation. This normally costs £35-75 per person sharing a double/twin room. Rates for solo travellers are usually higher because they pay a single occupancy rate. Evening meals are usually available and the standard of food these days is fairly high. Many of the pubs serve a selection of local beers: for some, this is a highlight of the trek. Most pubs have their own websites.

Hotels: the hotels on offer range from basic ones to more luxury properties. Prices vary widely. They all provide 'Full English' breakfasts and most also offer evening meals. Most hotels have their own websites and many list their rooms on the generic travel booking sites such as expedia.com or booking.com.

Hostels: these offer beds in dormitories and sometimes private rooms. Generally, they will have shared bathrooms, self-catering kitchen facilities and communal areas. Continental breakfast (tea and toast) is sometimes available. Bedding is usually supplied. Like B&Bs, hostels are becoming more upmarket and prices rise along with the quality of the offering. A bed usually costs £20-30 per person. Groups of two or more may find B&Bs to be better value.

Bunkhouses & camping barns: these provide beds in dormitories. Quality varies and often the accommodation is very basic: you will usually need to bring your own sleeping bag. Sometimes there will be showers and self-catering facilities. Prices are low.

Camping

Staithes (Stage 6b/7a)

Camping is the cheapest way to hike the CLW: a pitch each night costs only £5-15 per person. It also usually offers more freedom because campsites rarely need to be booked far in advance (except during July/August and public holiday weekends) and you can often adjust your itinerary as you go. Some trekkers camp every night while others camp only for a few nights at a time and then head to a B&B for a spot of relative luxury. There are plenty of commercial campsites close to the route.

Normally campsites are clean and well-maintained but a few (usually those on remote farms) are very basic. Showers are normally provided but you may pay a little extra for this luxury. Even if you have booked in advance, it is always sensible to telephone at least a day or two beforehand so that the campsite knows when to expect you. To help campers plan, we have set out below a list of campsites along the CLW. Contact details and information on facilities are provided in the full Accommodation Listings (see pages 23 to 31).

As regards wild camping, legally you require landowner consent. Much of the route is within the NYMNP where almost all the land is privately owned and the landowners are often local farmers. If you do wish to wild camp, then legally you should ask for the relevant farmer's permission. Some may allow it but others do not welcome wild campers. Some CLW trekkers do camp wild (without consent) by being discreet and pitching up late. However, we cannot condone this and, because there is so much open terrain along the CLW, concealment is difficult. During the Covid-19 pandemic, the number of wild campers throughout the UK increased dramatically and it is therefore more important than ever to respect the land and the landowners' wishes.

The obvious downside to camping is that you need to carry a lot more gear: tents, sleeping mats, sleeping bags and stoves all add weight to your pack, making the trek more difficult. In the 'Equipment' section, we provide advice on how to lighten your load. However, another solution is to use a baggage transfer service to transfer your heavy bags between campsites (see 'Baggage transfer').

Stage		Campsite
1a Helmsley	7	YHA Helmsley
1a/1b Scawton (0.7 miles OR)	9	Bungdale Head Farm Campsite
1b/2a (1.1-1.4 miles OR)	11	Wethercote Farm Campsite
2b/2c High Paradise Farm	15	High Paradise Farm
2c/3a Osmotherley (0.3 miles OR)	20	Cote Ghyll Caravan & Camping Park
3a/3b Lordstones	23	Lordstones
3b/4 (0.5 miles OR)	24	Beak Hills Farm
4/5a Kildale	28	Kildale Camping & Barn
5b/5c Slapewath (0.7 miles OR)	32	Margrove Park
6a/6b Skinningrove (0.3 miles OR)	41	Magpie Wood Caravans & Glamping
7a/7b Hinderwell (0.6 miles OR)	47	Serenity Camping
7b/7c Runswick Bay	51	Runswick Bay Caravan & Camping Park
7c/7d Lythe (1 mile OR)	53	Lythe Caravan and Camping
7e/8 Whitby	83	Folly Gardens Campsite
8/9a RHB (0.6 miles OR)	97	Middlewood Farm Holiday Park
8/9a RHB (0.4 miles OR)	99	Hooks House Farm
8/9a RHB (0.8 miles OR)	100	Bay Ness Farm
9b/9c Ravenscar (0.4 miles OR)	103	Bent Rigg Farm
9d Scalby Mills (0.5 miles OR)	107	Scarborough Camping and Caravanning Club site
10b Filey	128	Filey Brigg Camping & Caravan Site
10b Filey	140	Centenary Way Camping and Caravan Park

Accommodation Listings

- Dormitory
- Private Room
- Camping
- Drinks
- Lunch
- Evening Meals
- Breakfast
- Food shop
- WiFi
- OR Off-route

The Skipper Dora sculpture in Whitby

Stage		Name	Facilities	Contact Details
1a Helmsley	1	The Black Swan	Private Room, WiFi, Drinks, Breakfast, Lunch, Evening Meals	01439 770466 reservations@blackswan-helmsley.co.uk www.inncollectiongroup.com
1a Helmsley	2	Feathers Hotel	Private Room, WiFi, Drinks, Breakfast, Lunch, Evening Meals	01439 770275 feathers@innmail.co.ukwww.feathershotelhelmsley.co.uk
1a Helmsley	3	The Royal Oak	Private Room, WiFi, Drinks, Breakfast, Lunch, Evening Meals	01439 770450 royaloakhotelhelmsley@gmail.com www.royaloakhotelhelmsley.com
1a Helmsley	4	Feversham Arms Hotel	Private Room, WiFi, Drinks, Breakfast, Lunch, Evening Meals	01439 770766 stay@fevershamarmshotel.com www.fevershamarmshotel.com
1a Helmsley	5	Orchard Cottage B&B	Private Room, WiFi, Breakfast	07770 867678 info@orchardcottagehelmsley.co.uk www.orchardcottagehelmsley.co.uk
1a Helmsley	6	Helmsley Garden Cottage & Railway Carriage	Private Room, WiFi	01439 771864 louise@onebondgate.com www.onebondgate.com
1a Helmsley	7	YHA Helmsley	Private Room, Dormitory, Camping, WiFi, Drinks, Breakfast	0345 3719638 helmsley@yha.org.uk www.yha.org.uk
1a Helmsley	8	Stilworth House	Private Room, WiFi, Breakfast	01439 771072 carol@stilworth.co.uk www.stilworth.co.uk
1a/1b Scawton (0.7 miles OR)	9	Bungdale Head Farm Campsite	Camping	01439 770589/07792 790434 sm.foster@hotmail.co.uk www.bungdaleheadcamping.co.uk
1a/1b Scawton (1.1 miles OR)	10	The Hare Inn	Private Room, WiFi, Drinks, Breakfast, Evening Meals	01845 597769 harereservations@gmail.com www.thehare-inn.com
1b/2a (1.1-1.4 miles OR)	11	Wethercote Farm Campsite	Camping	07516 135303/07866 299313 fliss@wethercotefarmcampsite.com www.wethercotefarmcampsite.com

Stage		Name	Facilities	Contact Details
1c/2a Kilburn (1.2 miles OR)	12	The Forresters Arms		01904 947570 info@forresterskilburn.co.uk www.forresterskilburn.co.uk
1c/2a Kilburn (1.2 miles OR)	13	Church Farm B&B		01347 868318 carol@churchfarmkilburn.co.uk www.churchfarmkilburn.co.uk
2a/2b Boltby (1 mile OR)	14	Willow Tree Cottage B&B		01845 537406 townsend.willowtreecottage@gmail.com www.willowtreecottageboltby.co.uk
2b/2c High Paradise Farm	15	High Paradise Farm		07739 498255 info@highparadise.co.uk www.highparadise.co.uk **Breakfast hamper/dinner to be booked in advance**
2c/3a Osmotherley	16	Queen Catherine Hotel		01609 883209 www.queencatherinehotel.co.uk
2c/3a Osmotherley	17	The Golden Lion		01609 883526 info@goldenlionosmotherley.co.uk www.goldenlionosmotherley.co.uk
2c/3a Osmotherley	18	The Three Tuns		01609 883301
2c/3a Osmotherley	19	Vane House B&B		01609 883406
2c/3a Osmotherley (0.3 miles OR)	20	Cote Ghyll Caravan & Camping Park		01609 883425 hills@coteghyll.com www.coteghyll.com
2c/3a Osmotherley (0.4 miles OR)	21	Cote Ghyll Mill Youth Hostel		01609 883425 mill@coteghyll.com www.coteghyll.com
Stage 3a (0.6 miles OR)	22	Park House Country Guest House		01609 882899 www.parkhousecountryguesthouse.com
3a/3b Lordstones	23	Lordstones		01642 778482 info@lordstones.com www.lordstones.com
3b/4 (0.5 miles OR)	24	Beak Hills Farm		01642 778371 booking@beakhillsfarm.co.uk www.beakhillsfarm.co.uk
3b/4 Great Broughton (2 miles OR)	25	The Wainstones Hotel		01642 712268 reception@wainstoneshotel.co.uk www.wainstoneshotel.co.uk
3b/4 Great Broughton (2 miles OR)	26	Newlands House B&B		01642 712619

Stage		Name	Facilities	Contact Details
3b/4 Great Broughton (2 miles OR)	27	Dromonby Bridge B&B		01642 712226
4/5a Kildale	28	Kildale Camping & Barn		01642 722847 barnandcamping@kildalebarn.co.uk www.kildalebarn.co.uk
5a/5b Newton-under-Roseberry (0.8 miles OR)	29	King's Head Inn		01642 032780 info@kingsheadinn.co.uk www.inncollectiongroup.com
5a/5b Newton-under-Roseberry (1.5 miles OR)	30	Pinchinthorpe Hall		01287 213250 info@pinchinthorpehall.com www.pinchinthorpehall.com
5b/5c Slapewath	31	Fox and Hound Hotel		01287 635280 bookings@foxandhoundhotel.com www.foxandhoundhotel.com
5b/5c Slapewath (0.7 miles OR)	32	Margrove Park		01287 653616 margrovepark@btconnect.com www.margroveparkholidays.co.uk
5c/5d Skelton Green	33	Westerlands Guest House		01287 650690
5d/5e Skelton	34	Wharton Arms Hotel		01287 650618
5e/6a Saltburn-by-the-Sea	35	The Victoria Pub		01287 626131
5e/6a Saltburn-by-the-Sea	36	The Spa Hotel		01287 622544 www.thespahotelsaltburn.co.uk
5e/6a Saltburn-by-the-Sea	37	Brockley Hall Hotel		01287 622179 reception@brockleyhallhotel.com www.brockleyhallhotel.com
5e/6a Saltburn-by-the-Sea	38	Saltburn House B&B		01287 622008 info@saltburnhouse.co.uk www.saltburnhouse.co.uk
5e/6a Saltburn-by-the-Sea	39	Victorian Guest House		01287 625237
6a/6b Skinningrove	40	Moonfleet Guesthouse		07572 743951 moonfleetguesthouse@icloud.com www.moonfleetguesthouse.co.uk
6a/6b Skinningrove (0.3 miles OR)	41	Magpie Wood Caravans & Glamping		07444 288058
6b Boulby	42	Alum House Luxury B&B		07530 453470 alumhousebandb@yahoo.co.uk www.alumhouseluxurybandb.co.uk
6b/7a Staithes	43	The Endeavour B&B		01947 841029 www.endeavour-restaurant.co.uk **Dinner only available occasionally**

Stage		Name	Facilities	Contact Details
6b/7a Staithes	44	The Royal George		01947 841432 royalgeorgestaithes@gmail.com www.theroyalgeorgestaithes.co.uk
6b/7a Staithes	45	Captain Cook Inn		01947 840200 thecaptaincookinn@gmail.com www.captaincookinn.co.uk
6b/7a Staithes	46	Roraima House		01947 841423 www.bedandbreakfast-staithes.co.uk
7a/7b Hinderwell (0.6 miles OR)	47	Serenity Camping		01947 841122 hello@serenitycamping.co.uk www.serenitycamping.co.uk
7a/7b Hinderwell (0.6 miles OR)	48	St Hilda's Complex		01947 841243 info@sthildascomplex.co.uk www.sthildascomplex.co.uk
7a/7b Hinderwell (0.6 miles OR)	49	The Brown Cow pub		01947 840694
7b/7c Runswick Bank Top	50	Runswick Bay Hotel		01947 841010 www.therunswickbay.com
7b/7c Runswick Bank Top	51	Runswick Bay Caravan & Camping Park		01947 840997 runswickbaycaravanandcampingpark.co.uk
7b/7c Runswick Bank Top	52	The Firs Guesthouse		01947 840433 info@the-firs.co.uk www.the-firs.co.uk **2 night booking normally required**
7c/7d Lythe (1 mile OR)	53	Lythe Caravan and Camping		07496 987688 info@thestiddy.co.uk www.thestiddy.co.uk
7c/7d Lythe (1 mile OR)	54	The Stiddy pub		01947 893295 info@thestiddy.co.uk www.thestiddy.co.uk
7d/7e Sandsend	55	The Beach Hotel		01947 893200 www.beachhotelsandsend.co.uk
7d/7e Sandsend	56	Estbek House Hotel		01947 893424 estbekbooking@gmail.com www.estbekhouse.co.uk
7d/7e Sandsend	57	The Woodlands Hotel		01947 893899 hello@thewoodlandssandsend.co.uk www.thewoodlandssandsend.co.uk
7d/7e Sandsend	58	Mulgrave Country Cottage B&B		01947 893680 bookings@mulgravecountrycottage.co.uk www.mulgravecountrycottage.co.uk
7e (0.4 miles OR)	59	Raithwaite		01947 661661 reservations@raithwaite.com www.raithwaitesandsend.co.uk
7e (1 mile OR)	60	Dunsley Hall Hotel		01947 893437 reception@dunsleyhall.com www.dunsleyhall.com
7e/8 Whitby	61	Seacliffe Hotel		01947 603139 stay@seacliffehotel.com www.seacliffehotel.com

Stage		Name	Facilities	Contact Details
7e/8 Whitby	62	The Wheeldale		01947 602365 www.wheeldale-hotel.co.uk
7e/8 Whitby	63	Morningside Hotel		01947 604030 morningside@btconnect.com www.morningsidehotelwhitby.co.uk
7e/8 Whitby	64	Saxonville Hotel		01947 602631 newtons@saxonville.co.uk www.saxonville.co.uk
7e/8 Whitby	65	Haven Crest B&B		01947 605187 enquiries@havencrest.co.uk www.havencrest.co.uk
7e/8 Whitby	66	Riviera Guesthouse		01947 602533 info@rivierawhitby.com www.rivierawhitby.com
7e/8 Whitby	67	The Royal Hotel		0330 094 5919 www.bespokehotels.com
7e/8 Whitby	68	La Rosa Hotel		01947 606981 info@larosa.co.uk www.larosa.co.uk
7e/8 Whitby	69	The Pier Inn		01947 605284 www.thepierwhitby.co.uk
7e/8 Whitby	70	The Station Inn		01947 600498 thestationinn.whitby@ stonegategroup.co.uk www.greatukpubs.co.uk
7e/8 Whitby	71	The Marine Hotel		www.the-marine-hotel.co.uk
7e/8 Whitby	72	The Granby		01947 601747 granby.whitby@hotmail.com www.granbywhitby.co.uk
7e/8 Whitby	73	Sandpiper House B&B		01947 600246 enquiries@sandpiperhouse.co.uk www.sandpiperhouse.co.uk
7e/8 Whitby	74	No.7 Guesthouse		01947 606019 number7.whitbytown@btinternet.com www.numbersevenguesthouse.co.uk
7e/8 Whitby	75	Harrys		01947 601909 www.harrysloungebar.co.uk
7e/8 Whitby	76	The Corner Guesthouse		01947 602444 info@thecornerguesthouse.co.uk www.thecornerguesthouse.co.uk
7e/8 Whitby	77	Ellies Guesthouse		01947 600022 info@elliesguesthouse.co.uk www.elliesguesthouse.co.uk
7e/8 Whitby	78	The Angel Hotel		01947 824730 www.jdwetherspoon.com
7e/8 Whitby	79	YHA Whitby		0345 371 9049 whitby@yha.org.uk www.yha.org.uk

Stage		Name	Facilities	Contact Details
7e/8 Whitby	80	The Dolphin		01947 821455 www.thedolphinwhitby.co.uk
7e/8 Whitby	81	The White Horse & Griffin		01947 604857 info@whitehorseandgriffin.com www.whitehorseandgriffin.com
7e/8 Whitby	82	The Endeavour pub		01947 603557 endeavourwhitby@icloud.com www.endeavourpub.co.uk
7e/8 Whitby	83	Folly Gardens Campsite		01947 601364 follygardenslive@gmail.com www.follygardens-whitby.co.uk
8/9a RHB	84	Thackwood B&B		01947 880858 enquiries@thackwood.com www.thackwood.com
8/9a RHB	85	Manning Tree B&B		01947 881042 themanningtree@btinternet.com www.manningtreebnb.co.uk
8/9a RHB	86	Fernleigh B&B		01947 880523 fernleigh_rhb@icloud.com www.fernleigh-robin-hoods-bay.co.uk
8/9a RHB	87	Lee-Side B&B		01947 881143 cj.leeside@outlook.com www.lee-side.co.uk
8/9a RHB	88	Aldersyde B&B		01947 880689 info@aldersyde-robinhoodsbay.co.uk www.aldersyde-robinhoodsbay.co.uk
8/9a RHB	89	The Villa B&B		01947 881043
8/9a RHB	90	The Grosvenor Hotel		01947 880320 grosvenor.bay@gmail.com www.thegrosvenor.info
8/9a RHB	91	Wayfarer Guest House & Bistro		01947 880240 thewayfarerbistro@outlook.com www.wayfarer-robinhoodsbay.co.uk
8/9a RHB	92	West Royd B&B		01947 880678/07729 479618 westroydbnb@gmail.com www.westroyd.co.uk
8/9a RHB	93	Birtley House B&B		01947 880566 birtleyhouserhb@gmail.com
8/9a RHB	94	The Victoria Hotel		01947 880205 www.victoriarhb.com
8/9a RHB	95	Smugglers Bistro Bar		01947 880099 info@smugglersrhb.co.uk www.boathouserhb.co.uk
8/9a RHB	96	Bay Hotel		01947 880278 www.bayhotel.info
8/9a RHB (0.6 miles OR)	97	Middlewood Farm Holiday Park		01947 880414 www.middlewoodfarm.com
8/9a RHB (1 mile OR)	98	Thorpe Green House B&B		01947 880339 www.thorpegreen.co.uk

Stage		Name	Facilities	Contact Details
8/9a RHB (0.4 miles OR)	99	Hooks House Farm		01947 880283 www.hookshousefarm.co.uk
8/9a RHB (0.8 miles OR)	100	Bay Ness Farm		baynessfarm@baynessfarm.co.uk www.baynessfarm.co.uk
9a/9b Boggle Hole	101	YHA Boggle Hole		0345 371 9504 bogglehole@yha.org.uk www.yha.org.uk
9b/9c Ravenscar	102	Raven Hall Country House Hotel		01723 870353 enquiries@ravenhall.co.uk www.ravenhall.co.uk
9b/9c Ravenscar (0.4 miles OR)	103	Bent Rigg Farm		01723 870475/07875 458048 juliebentrigg@gmail.com www.bentriggfarmcampsite.co.uk
9c/9d Hayburn Wyke (0.3 miles OR)	104	The Hayburn Wyke Inn		01723 870202 www.hayburnwykeinn.co.uk
9d Cloughton (1.2 miles OR)	105	The Blacksmiths Arms Inn		01723 870244 info@blacksmithsarmsinn.co.uk www.blacksmithsarmsinn.co.uk
9d Burniston (1.3 miles OR)	106	The Oak Wheel pub		01723 870230 enquiries@theoakwheel.com www.theoakwheel.com
9d Scalby Mills (0.5 miles OR)	107	Scarborough Camping and Caravanning Club site		01723 366212 www.campingandcaravanningclub.co.uk
9d Scalby Mills (0.5 miles OR)	108	YHA Scarborough		0345 260 2896 scarborough@yha.org.uk www.yha.org.uk
9d/10a Scarborough	109	Clifton Hotel		www.britanniahotels.com
9d/10a Scarborough	110	Premier Inn Scarborough (North Bay)		0330 128 1344 www.premierinn.com
9d/10a Scarborough	111	The Alexander		01723 363178 www.alexanderhotelscarborough.co.uk
9d/10a Scarborough	112	The Headlands Hotel		01723 373717 info@theheadlandshotel.co.uk www.theheadlandshotel.co.uk
9d/10a Scarborough	113	Norlands B&B		01723 658089/07936 042061 info@norlandshotel.co.uk www.norlandshotel.co.uk
9d/10a Scarborough	114	Howdale B&B		01723 372696 mail@howdalehotel.co.uk www.howdalehotel.co.uk
9d/10a Scarborough	115	Leeway Hotel		01723 374371 info@leewayhotel.co.uk www.leewayhotel.co.uk

Stage		Name	Facilities	Contact Details
9d/10a Scarborough	116	The Helaina B&B		01723 375191 info@hotelhelaina.co.uk www.thehelaina.co.uk
9d/10a Scarborough	117	Marine View Guest House		01723 361864 info@marineview.co.uk www.marineview.co.uk
9d/10a Scarborough	118	Castle By The Sea B&B		01723 365166 www.thecastlebythesea.co.uk
9d/10a Scarborough	119	Tall Storeys		01723 373696 info@tallstoreyshotel.co.uk www.tallstoreyshotel.co.uk
9d/10a Scarborough	120	Royal Hotel		www.britanniahotels.com
9d/10a Scarborough	121	Travelodge Scarborough		08719 846430 www.travelodge.co.uk
9d/10a Scarborough	122	The Grand Hotel		www.britanniahotels.com
9d/10a Scarborough	123	Boat Shed Hostel		07889 180925/07779 974333 paula@boatshedhostel.co.uk www.boatshedhostel.co.uk
9d/10a Scarborough	124	Bike & Boot		01723 655555 bookings.scarborough@bikeandboot.com www.bikeandboot.com
9d/10a Scarborough	125	The Highlander		www.thehighlander.inn.fan
9d/10a Scarborough	126	Mansion House		01723 373930 info@mansionhousehotel.com www.mansionhousescarborough.co.uk
10a/10b Cayton (1 mile OR)	127	The Farrier		01723 861432 enquiry@the-farrier.co.uk www.the-farrier.co.uk
10b Filey	128	Filey Brigg Camping & Caravan Site		01723 513852 fileybrigg.sca@northyorks.gov.uk www.fileybriggcaravanpark.co.uk
10b Filey	129	Three Tuns Hotel		01723 512183 threetunshotel@gmail.com www.threetunsfiley.co.uk
10b Filey	130	Binton Guesthouse		01723 513753 contact@bintonguesthouse.co.uk www.bintonguesthouse.co.uk
10b Filey	131	Filey Grange Guesthouse		01723 513396 luis.hewitt@hotmail.com www.fileygrange.co.uk
10b Filey	132	The Forge Guesthouse		01723 514646 wendyandgarethhand@gmail.com www.theforgefiley.com
10b Filey	133	Beachdale Guesthouse		01723 317560 stay@beachdalefiley.co.uk www.beachdalefiley.co.uk

Stage		Name	Facilities	Contact Details
10b Filey	134	All Seasons Guesthouse		01723 515321 enquiries@allseasonsboutiquehotels.com www.allseasonsboutiquehotels.com
10b Filey	135	White Rose Guest House		01723 516337 www.whiterosefiley.co.uk
10b Filey	136	White Lodge Hotel		01723 514771 reception@whitelodgehotelfiley.co.uk www.whitelodgehotelfiley.co.uk
10b Filey	137	Atholl Guesthouse		01723 515189 www.athol-guesthouse.co.uk
10b Filey	138	Rutland West Guesthouse		01723 514750 enquiries@rutlandwestfiley.co.uk www.rutlandwestfiley.co.uk
10b Filey	139	Daffodil Guest House		01723 671498 daffodil.filey@gmail.com www.daffodilguesthousefiley.com
10b Filey	140	Centenary Way Camping and Caravan Park		01723 516415 www.centenarywaycamping.co.uk

Booking Tips

- The CLW becomes more popular each year. To ensure that you secure your accommodation of choice, book as early as you can. Many trekkers start booking in autumn (just after the current summer season has ended) for the following season.
- Try to book 'hot-spots' first: generally, these are places where there are only a few accommodation options. Once you have secured the accommodation which books up most quickly, you can normally slot in the rest of your accommodation more easily. If you leave hot-spots until last then you might have to unwind and rebook other reservations if any hot-spots that you desire are unavailable.
- Start mid-week. A large number of trekkers start the trail at the weekend. Those who start mid-week are often 'out of sync' with the bulk of the trekkers and may therefore find accommodation more easily.
- Weekends are normally busier (even in low season).
- If you cannot find accommodation along the CLW itself, try looking for beds in towns/villages a few miles away.
- Those who hike alone, or in pairs, will find it easiest to find beds. For larger groups, it is more difficult.
- If you cannot secure the accommodation that you need then contact one of the unguided tour companies or accommodation booking services. Often they block-book accommodation in advance and may have spaces.
- Occasionally, the last-minute booker can get lucky: tour companies which pre-book in blocks will release unsold beds a few weeks or months before the relevant dates. If you call a few weeks before your trip, you may be lucky enough to bag some beds which have just been released.

Facilities

Stage	Place	Private Rooms	Camping	Dormitory Beds	Meals/ Drinks	Grocery Shop	Transport
1a	Helmsley	✓	✓	✓	✓	✓	✓
1a	Rievaulx Abbey (0.5 miles OR)				✓		✓
1a/1b	Scawton (0.7-1.1 miles OR)	✓	✓		✓		
1c/2a	Kilburn (1.2 miles OR)	✓			✓		✓
2a	Sutton Bank				✓		✓
2a/2b	Boltby (1 mile OR)	✓					
2b/2c	High Paradise Farm	✓	✓		✓		
2c/3a	Osmotherley	✓	✓	✓	✓	✓	✓
3a/3b	Lordstones	✓	✓		✓	✓	
3b/4	Great Broughton (2-3 miles OR)	✓			✓		✓
3b/4	Beak Hills Farm (0.5 miles OR)	✓	✓		✓ (Residents)		
4	Clay Bank Top						✓

Stage	Place	Private Rooms	Camping	Dormitory Beds	Meals/ Drinks	Grocery Shop	Transport
4/5a	Kildale		▲	🛏			🚆
5a/5b	Newton-under-Roseberry (0.8-1.5 miles OR)	🔑			🍴🍷		🚌
5b/5c	Slapewath	🔑	▲ OR		🍴🍷		🚌 OR
5c/5d	Skelton Green	🔑			🍴🍷		
5d/5e	Skelton	🔑			🍴🍷	🛒	🚌
5e/6a	Saltburn-by-the-Sea	🔑			🍴🍷	🛒	🚆 🚌
6a/6b	Skinningrove	🔑	▲ OR		🍴🍷	🛒	🚌
6b	Boulby	🔑					🚌
6b/7a	Staithes	🔑			🍴🍷	🛒	🚌
7a/7b	Port Mulgrave/ Hinderwell (0.4-0.7 miles OR)	🔑	▲		🍴🍷		🚌
7b/7c	Runswick Bay	🔑	▲		🍴🍷		🚌
7c/7d	Lythe (1 mile OR)	🔑	▲		🍴🍷	🛒	🚌

Stage	Place	Private Rooms	Camping	Dormitory Beds	Meals/ Drinks	Grocery Shop	Transport
7d/7e	Sandsend	✓			✓	✓	✓
7e/8	Whitby	✓	✓		✓	✓	✓ ✓
8/9a	Robin Hood's Bay	✓	✓		✓	✓	✓
9a/9b	Boggle Hole	✓		✓	✓		
9b/9c	Ravenscar	✓	✓		✓	✓	✓
9c/9d	Hayburn Wyke Inn (0.3 miles OR)	✓			✓		
9d	Cloughton (1.2 miles OR)	✓			✓		✓
9d	Burniston (1.3 miles OR)	✓			✓		✓
9d	Scalby Mills (0.5 miles OR)	✓	✓	✓	✓		
9d/10a	Scarborough	✓		✓	✓	✓	✓ ✓
10a/10b	Cayton (1 mile OR)	✓			✓	✓	✓
10b	Filey	✓	✓		✓	✓	✓ ✓

Food

Approaching Runswick Bay (Stage 7c)

Breakfast: for many trekkers, breakfast will be provided as part of the overnight package at B&Bs, pubs or hotels. Normally, this will be a 'Full English' breakfast which is a large helping of bacon, sausage, eggs, mushrooms and black pudding. However, healthier options are usually available too.

Lunch: almost all accommodation providers can prepare a packed lunch for you. Be sure to request this the night before. Alternatively, on some stages, you can stop for lunch at a pub or café along the route. We have marked on the maps isolated pubs/cafés located mid-stage: however, at overnight stops, there are too many pubs/cafés to mark them on the maps.

Evening meals: if your accommodation does not offer evening meals then the staff will usually be able to recommend a pub/restaurant within walking distance or provide details of a nearby takeaway business which will deliver an evening meal. They may even give you a lift to a nearby pub in the evening: check when booking. Most villages have a pub/inn, serving food and excellent beer. In fact, for many hikers, the 'pub grub' and 'real ale' are highlights of the trek: the beers available are some of England's finest.

Self-catering: sadly, many rural shops have closed down in recent years and this trend seems likely to continue. However, there are still many grocery shops and small supermarkets that serve the CLW and they are listed in the route descriptions. Some of the shops are in towns/villages which the trail actually enters. However, other shops are a short distance OR. Often the shops are small with a limited range of products but, as long as you are not too fussy, you should find plenty to eat. However, if you are more particular, or you have specific nutritional requirements, you may wish to stock up on supplies before setting out on the trek. Plan ahead so you know where your next re-supply point is.

However, remember that food is heavy so you will not be able to start the trek carrying all the food that you will require for the full distance. It is much better to accept at the outset that you can only carry a few days' food than to exhaust yourself in the early stages of the trek by carrying too much. Many campers carry only a small amount of food which they supplement with meals at pubs and cafés along the way. It is sensible to carry dried food (such as pasta and rice): water is food's heaviest component. Pre-packed freeze-dried meals for backpackers are an excellent choice because they are light and are prepared simply by adding boiling water.

Travel

Travel to England

There are numerous airports in the UK with plenty of domestic and international flights. The closest international airports to the CLW are Teesside (Darlington), Leeds-Bradford, Manchester, Liverpool, Birmingham and Newcastle. There are trains from each of these cities (and sometimes the airports themselves) to various destinations throughout England, including Filey (the E trail-head) and York which has a bus connection to Helmsley (the W trail-head). Teesside Airport is only a stone's throw from the NYMNP and nearby Darlington has rail links to Saltburn (Stage 5e/6a). Manchester Airport is convenient too because there are direct trains between the airport itself and York. There are also rail services between Birmingham Airport and York but you will have to change trains.

Further away, there are the various London airports (London City, London Luton, London Heathrow, London Stansted and London Gatwick) which have a wide variety of domestic and international flights: from each airport, there are bus/train connections to Northern England but sometimes you will first need to travel into the centre of London. Scotland also has international airports at Glasgow and Edinburgh.

Travel to/from the primary trail-heads

Those walking W-E will start at Helmsley. Those walking E-W will start at Filey.

By public transport:

Helmsley: because Helmsley has no train station, most trekkers arriving on public transport will come by bus from York or Scarborough. Available services include:

- **Reliance bus 31X**: operates between York and Helmsley (75min; 3 times/day; Mon-Sat; www.reliancebuses.co.uk)
- **Moorsbus bus M31**: operates between York and Helmsley (80min; Summer Sundays and public holidays; www.moorsbus.org)
- **East Yorkshire Buses 128**: operates between Helmsley and Scarborough (105min daily; www.eastyorkshirebuses.co.uk)

Both York and Scarborough are well connected to the rest of the UK by rail. You can also travel by coach between Scarborough or York and other UK cities including London, Birmingham, Leeds and Sheffield: see **www.nationalexpress.com** and **www.uk.megabus.com**.

Filey: Northern Rail trains between Hull and Scarborough stop at Filey. Hull and Scarborough are both well connected to the rest of the UK by rail. To check train times and buy tickets, see **www.thetrainline.com**. You can also travel by coach between Scarborough or Hull and other UK cities including London, Birmingham, Leeds and Sheffield: **see www.nationalexpress.com**.

By car: you can park your car in Helmsley or Filey and use public transport to return to it at the end of the trek: see 'Travel between Helmsley and Filey'. If you are staying at a hotel/B&B in Helmsley or Filey, they may let you park your car long-term for a fee: check when booking.

Helmsley: you can park for free along some of the town's streets provided of course that you can find a space. Alternatively, you can park in the Cleveland Way Car Park (just N of Helmsley Castle): you can buy 7/10 day permits online at **www.northyorks.gov.uk** (£23/33). Permits can be posted to you for a small additional fee or you can pick them up from Porters Coffee Shop or the ticket office at Helmsley Castle. If you are travelling by camper-van, there is another parking area (beside the Cleveland Way Car Park) where you are permitted to sleep overnight in your van (free of charge).

Filey: you can park for free along some of the town's streets provided of course that you can find a space. Alternatively, you can park in one of four long-stay car parks managed by North Yorkshire Council: you can buy advance parking permits for 2-7 days (£8/day) by contacting the council (see **www.northyorks.gov.uk**). This advance parking permit can also be used in council long-stay car parks in Scarborough, RHB, Whitby, Sandsend, Runswick Bay and Staithes. However, the process of requesting the permit is a bit time-consuming and permits must be picked up in Scarborough or Whitby so it is not the simplest way to organise your parking. It is much easier to pay for council parking in Filey using the **RingGo** smartphone app. The Country Park car park near Filey Brigg costs around £9/day on the app: you can only pay for a maximum of 7 days at one time but this can be extended.

By taxi: taxi operators serving Helmsley and/or Filey are highlighted in red in the list on p40.

Travel between Filey and Helmsley

If you leave a car or luggage at your start point, you can use public transport to return to it at the end of the trek. Trains travel regularly between Filey and Scarborough (20min; daily; **www.thetrainline.com**). There are also buses between Filey and Scarborough: see 'Public Transport along the CLW'. From Scarborough Railway Station, East Yorkshire Buses No.128 can take you to Helmsley (105min; daily; **www.eastyorkshirebuses.co.uk**).

Public transport along the CLW

Train: there are mainline train stations at Kildale (Stage 4/5a), Saltburn-by-the-Sea (Stage 5e/6a), Whitby (Stage 7e/8), Scarborough (Stage 9d/10a) and Filey (Stage 10b). From each of these stations, you can travel to many destinations around the UK, although you may have to change trains. For further information, see **www.thetrainline.com**.

In addition, the North Yorkshire Moors Railway, a volunteer operated heritage steam railway, runs during the main hiking season between Whitby and the historic market town of Pickering. It stops at some wonderful old heritage stations along the way including Grosmont and Goathland (which was the setting for Hogsmeade Station in the first Harry Potter film). Travelling by steam train is a wonderful experience and it is lovely to take time out from hiking for a side-trip. For tickets, timetables and further information, see **www.nymr.co.uk**.

Buses: there are numerous bus services that are useful to the CLW trekker. Many stop at places along the CLW. In this book, we refer to these places (other than the primary trail-heads at Helmsley and Filey) as 'secondary trail-heads' and there is a list of them on pages 42 to 45, together with details of the relevant transport options: these services can be useful if you need to abandon the trek for any reason or if you wish to skip a stage or two. They can also assist if you are only intending to walk part of the CLW: see 'Hiking shorter sections of the CLW'. The key services operating close to the CLW are set out below. There are too many bus services operating in the region to list them all.

Bus Service	Key Information (Places in red have a mainline train station)
Arriva 3/X3/X3A (Mon-Sat)	**Skelton** (Stage 5d/5e) - **Saltburn** (Stage 5e/6a)
Arriva X4/X4A (Mon-Sat)	**Whitby** (Stage 7e/8) - **Sandsend** (Stage 7d/7e) - **Lythe** (Stage 7c/7d; 1 mile OR) - **Runswick Bank Top** (Stage 7b/7c; OR) - **Hinderwell** (Stage 7a/7b; 0.4 miles OR) - **Staithes** (Stage 6b/7a) - **Boulby** (Stage 6b) - **Easington** - **Saltburn** (Stage 5e/6a) - **Skelton** (Stage 5d/5e) - **Redcar** - **Middlesborough**
Arriva 5/5A (Mon-Sat)	**Middlesborough** - **Skelton** (Stage 5d/5e) - **Guisborough** - **Skinningrove** (Stage 6a/6b) - **Easington**
Arriva X93 (daily)	**Middlesborough** - **Guisborough** - **Charltons** (near Slapewath; Stage 5b/5c) - **Whitby** (Stage 7e/8) - **RHB** (Stage 8/9a) - **Scarborough** (Stage 9d/10a)
Coastliner 840/843 (daily)	**Leeds** - **York** - **Malton** - **Pickering** (840) - **Whitby** (Stage 7e/8; 840) - **Scarborough** (Stage 9d/10a; 843)
Coatham Coaches 18 (Mon-Fri)	**Stokesley** - **Newton-under-Roseberry** (Stage 5a/5b; 0.8 miles OR) - **Guisborough**
Coatham Coaches 80 (Mon-Sat)	**Stokesley** - **Ingleby Cross** - **Osmotherley** (Stage 2c/3a) - **Northallerton**
Coatham Coaches 89 (Mon-Sat)	**Stokesley** - **Great Broughton** (Stage 3b/4; 2 miles OR) - **Ingleby Cross** - **Osmotherley** (Stage 2c/3a) - **Northallerton**
East Yorkshire Buses 10 (daily)	**Scarborough** (Stage 9d/10a) - **Cayton** (Stage 10a/10b; 1 mile OR)
East Yorkshire Buses 12/13 (daily)	**Scarborough** (Stage 9d/10a) - **Cayton** (Stage 10a/10b; 1 mile OR) - **Filey** (Stage 10b) - **Bridlington**
East Yorkshire Buses 115 (Mon-Sat)	**Scarborough** (Stage 9d/10a) - **Burniston** (9d; 1.3 miles OR) - **Cloughton** (9d; 1.2 miles OR) - **Ravenscar** (Stage 9b/9c)
East Yorkshire Buses 128 (daily)	**Scarborough** (Stage 9d/10a) - **Pickering** - **Helmsley** (Stage 1a)
Moorsbus M3 (Summer weekends/ Public holidays)	**Darlington** - **Middlesborough** - **Guisborough** - **Danby** - **Castleton** - **Blakey Ridge** - **Helmsley** (Stage 1a) - **Pickering**
Moorsbus M4 (Summer weekends/ Public holidays)	**Saltburn** (Stage 5e/6a) - **Redcar** - **Guisborough** - **Stokesley** - **Great Broughton** (Stage 3b/4; 2 miles OR) - **Clay Bank Top** (Stage 4) - **Rievaulx Abbey** (Stage 1a; 0.5 miles OR) - **Helmsley** (Stage 1a) - **Sutton Bank** (Stage 2a)

Bus/Train Map
Route of trek
Train line
Arriva
Coastliner
Coatham Coaches
East Yorkshire
Moorbus M3
Moorbus M4
Moorbus M5
Moorbus M31/ Reliance 31X
North Yorkshire County Council
Shoreline Suncruiser
NORTH YORK MOORS
Darlington
Middlesbrough
Stockton-on-Tees
Teesside
Redcar
Stokesley
Northallerton
Thirsk
Saltburn-by-the-Sea
Skinningrove
Staithes
Port Mulgrave
Runswick Bay
Lythe exit
Sandsend
Whitby
Lythe
Hinderwell
Skelton
Slapewath
Guisborough
Danby
Kildale
Newton-under-Roseberry
Great Broughton
Great Broughton exit
Lordstones
Osmotherley
High Paradise Farm
Boltby exit
Scawton
Sutton Bank
Kilburn
Helmsley
Kirkbymoorside
Pickering
Goathland
Robin Hood's Bay
Boggle Hole
Ravenscar
Hayburn Wyke
Cloughton
Burniston
Scarborough
Cayton Bay
Cayton
Filey Brigg
Filey
3/X3/X3A/X4/X4A
X4/X4A
X93/5/5A
X93
M3
M4
M5
M31/31X
18
80
89
80/89
59
115
128
840
843
10/12/13
12/13

Bus Service	Key Information (Places in red have a mainline train station)
Moorsbus M5 (Summer weekends/ Public holidays)	Stockton - **Stokesley** - **Ingleby Cross** - Northallerton - Thirsk - **Helmsley** (Stage 1a)
Moorsbus M31 (Summer Sundays/ Public holidays)	York - **Helmsley** (Stage 1a)
North Yorkshire County Council 59 (Mon-Fri)	Thirsk - **Kilburn** (Stage 1c/2a)
Reliance Bus 31X (Mon-Sat)	York - **Helmsley** (Stage 1a)
Shoreline Suncruiser: Filey Flyer 555 (Mon-Sat)	Scarborough (Stage 9d/10a) - **Cayton Bay** (Stage 10a/10b) - Filey (Stage 10b)

Further information about bus travel:

Arriva: www.arrivabus.co.uk

Coastliner: www.transdevbus.co.uk; 01422 553576

Coatham Coaches: www.coathamcoaches.co.uk; 07947 950433

East Yorkshire Buses: www.eastyorkshirebuses.co.uk

Moorsbus: www.moorsbus.org; 01751 477216

North Yorkshire County Council: www.northyorkstravel.info

Reliance: www.reliancebuses.co.uk; info@reliancebuses.co.uk; 01904 768262

Shoreline Suncruisers: www.shorelinesuncruisers.co.uk; 01723 360969

Taxis: there are many taxi businesses operating from towns/villages near the CLW. They can often pick you up from the CLW, drive you to nearby accommodation and leave you back to the CLW the next morning. Some of them operate surprisingly far from their hubs. There are too many taxi businesses to list them all but many are set out below. Taxi operators serving Helmsley and/or Filey (the primary trail-heads) are highlighted in red.

- **York Cars Taxis** (York): www.yorkcars-taxis.co.uk; 01904 765765
- **Drive Taxis** (York): www.taxiyork.co.uk; 01904 659659
- **York Station Taxis** (York): www.yorkstationtaxis.co.uk; 01904 623332
- **Ryedale Taxis** (Helmsley/Thirsk/Malton): www.ryedaletaxis.com; 07795 807819
- **Helmsley Black Cabs** (Helmsley): 01439 223939
- **Station Taxis** (Malton): www.taxisinmalton.com; 01653 696969
- **Chapman's Taxis** (Thirsk): www.chapmanstaxis.co.uk; 01845 609957
- **KA Taxis** (Thirsk): www.ka-taxis.co.uk; 07817 858077
- **Al's Taxis** (Northallerton): www.alstaxisnorthallerton.co.uk; 07751 659372
- **Stokesley Taxis** (Stokesley): www.stokesleytaxis.co.uk; 01642 712999
- **Karis Taxis** (Kildale): www.karistravel. co.uk; 07398 941930
- **Frontline Taxis** (Guisborough): 01287 626260

- **Redcar Taxis** (Redcar): www.redcartaxis.co.uk; 01642 470470
- **Saltburn Taxis** (Saltburn): 01287 623567
- **White Rose Taxis** (Whitby): www.whiterosetaxis.co.uk; 01947 604604
- **Bay Private Hire** (RHB): www.bay-taxis.co.uk; 01947 880603
- **Nippy Taxis** (Scarborough): www.nippytaxis.co.uk; 01723 377377
- **Boro Cars** (Scarborough): www.boro-cars.com; 01723 361111
- **Cayton Cars** (Cayton): www.caytoncars.co.uk; 07760 585591
- **Radio Taxis** (Filey): www.take-a-taxi.co.uk; 01723 515515

Saltburn's famous water-balanced cliff lift (Stage 5e/6a)

Primary & Secondary trail-heads

Secondary Trail-head	Possible Destinations by Bus (Mainline train stations in red)	Bus/Train Services
1a Helmsley	**Blakey Ridge;** **Castleton** **Clay Bank Top** (Stage 4) **Danby** **Darlington** **Great Broughton** (Stage 3b/4; 2 miles OR) **Guisborough** **Ingleby Cross** **Middlesborough** **Northallerton** **Pickering** **Redcar** **Rievaulx Abbey** (Stage 1a; 0.5 miles OR) **Saltburn** (Stage 5e/6a) **Scarborough** (Stage 9d/10a) **Stockton** **Stokesley** **Sutton Bank** (Stage 2a) **Thirsk** **York**	East Yorkshire Buses 128 Moorsbus M3/M4/M5/M31 Reliance 31X
1a Rievaulx Abbey (0.5 miles OR)	**Clay Bank Top** (Stage 4) **Great Broughton** (Stage 3b/4; 2 miles OR) **Guisborough** **Helmsley** (Stage 1a) **Redcar** **Saltburn** (Stage 5e/6a) **Stokesley** **Sutton Bank** (Stage 2a)	Moorsbus M4
1c/2a Kilburn (1.2 miles OR)	**Thirsk**	North Yorkshire County Council 59
2a Sutton Bank	**Clay Bank Top** (Stage 4) **Great Broughton** (Stage 3b/4; 2 miles OR) **Guisborough** **Helmsley** (Stage 1a) **Redcar** **Stokesley** **Rievaulx Abbey** (Stage 1a; 0.5 miles OR) **Saltburn** (Stage 5e/6a)	Moorsbus M4
2c/3a Osmotherley	**Great Broughton** (Stage 3b/4; 2 miles OR) **Ingleby Cross** **Northallerton** **Stokesley**	Coatham Coaches 80/89
3b/4 Great Broughton (2 miles OR)	**Clay Bank Top** (Stage 4) **Guisborough** **Helmsley** (Stage 1a) **Ingleby Cross** **Northallerton** **Osmotherley** (Stage 2c/3a) **Redcar** **Rievaulx Abbey** (Stage 1a; 0.5 miles OR) **Saltburn** (Stage 5e/6a) **Stokesley** **Sutton Bank** (Stage 2a)	Moorsbus M4 Coatham Coaches 89
4 Clay Bank Top	**Great Broughton** (Stage 3b/4; 2 miles OR) **Guisborough** **Helmsley** (Stage 1a) **Redcar** **Rievaulx Abbey** (Stage 1a; 0.5 miles OR) **Saltburn** (Stage 5e/6a) **Stokesley** **Sutton Bank** (Stage 2a)	Moorsbus M4

Secondary Trail-head	Possible Destinations by Bus (Mainline train stations in red)	Bus/Train Services
4/5a **Kildale**	-	Train services
5a/5b **Newton-under-Roseberry** (0.8 miles OR)	**Guisborough** **Stokesley**	Coatham Coaches 18
5b/5c **Charltons** (near Slapewath)	**Guisborough** **Middlesborough** **RHB** (Stage 8/9a) **Scarborough** (Stage 9d/10a) **Whitby** (Stage 7e/8)	Arriva X93
5d/5e **Skelton**	**Boulby** (Stage 6b) **Easington** **Guisborough** **Hinderwell** (Stage 7a/7b; 0.4 miles OR) **Lythe** (Stage 7c/7d; 1 mile OR) **Middlesborough** **Redcar** **Runswick Bank Top** (Stage 7b/7c) **Saltburn** (Stage 5e/6a) **Sandsend** (Stage 7d/7e) **Skinningrove** (Stage 6a/6b) **Staithes** (Stage 6b/7a) **Whitby** (Stage 7e/8)	Arriva 3/X3/X3A Arriva X4/X4A Arriva 5/5A
5e/6a **Saltburn-by-the-Sea**	**Boulby** (Stage 6b) **Clay Bank Top** (Stage 4) **Easington** **Guisborough** **Helmsley** (Stage 1a) **Hinderwell** (Stage 7a/7b; 0.4 miles OR) **Great Broughton** (Stage 3b/4; 2 miles OR) **Lythe** (Stage 7c/7d; 1 mile OR) **Middlesborough** **Redcar** **Rievaulx Abbey** (Stage 1a; 0.5 miles OR) **Runswick Bank Top** (Stage 7b/7c) **Sandsend** (Stage 7d/7e) **Skelton** (Stage 5d/5e) **Staithes** (Stage 6b/7a) **Stokesley** **Sutton Bank** (Stage 2a) **Whitby** (Stage 7e/8)	Train services Arriva 3/X3/X3A Arriva X4/X4A Moorsbus M4
6a/6b **Skinningrove**	**Easington** **Guisborough** **Middlesborough** **Skelton** (Stage 5d/5e)	Arriva 5/5A
6b **Boulby**	**Easington** **Hinderwell** (Stage 7a/7b; 0.4 miles OR) **Lythe** (Stage 7c/7d; 1 mile OR) **Middlesborough** **Redcar** **Runswick Bank Top** (Stage 7b/7c) **Saltburn** (Stage 5e/6a) **Sandsend** (Stage 7d/7e) **Skelton** (Stage 5d/5e) **Staithes** (Stage 6b/7a) **Whitby** (Stage 7e/8)	Arriva X4/X4A

Secondary Trail-head	Possible Destinations by Bus (Mainline train stations in red)	Bus/Train Services
6b/7a Staithes	**Boulby** (Stage 6b) **Easington** **Hinderwell** (Stage 7a/7b; 0.4 miles OR) **Lythe** (Stage 7c/7d; 1 mile OR) **Middlesborough** **Redcar** **Runswick Bank Top** (Stage 7b/7c) **Saltburn** (Stage 5e/6a) **Sandsend** (Stage 7d/7e) **Skelton** (Stage 5d/5e) **Whitby** (Stage 7e/8)	Arriva X4/X4A
7a/7b Hinderwell (0.4 miles OR)	**Boulby** (Stage 6b) **Easington** **Lythe** (Stage 7c/7d; 1 mile OR) **Middlesborough** **Redcar** **Runswick Bank Top** (Stage 7b/7c) **Saltburn** (Stage 5e/6a) **Sandsend** (Stage 7d/7e) **Skelton** (Stage 5d/5e) **Staithes** (Stage 6b/7a) **Whitby** (Stage 7e/8)	Arriva X4/X4A
7b/7c Runswick Bank Top	**Boulby** (Stage 6b) **Easington** **Hinderwell** (Stage 7a/7b; 0.4 miles OR) **Lythe** (Stage 7c/7d; 1 mile OR) **Middlesborough** **Redcar** **Saltburn** (Stage 5e/6a) **Sandsend** (Stage 7d/7e) **Skelton** (Stage 5d/5e) **Staithes** (Stage 6b/7a) **Whitby** (Stage 7e/8)	Arriva X4/X4A
7c/7d Lythe (1 mile OR)	**Boulby** (Stage 6b) **Easington** **Hinderwell** (Stage 7a/7b; 0.4 miles OR) **Middlesborough** **Redcar** **Runswick Bank Top** (Stage 7b/7c) **Saltburn** (Stage 5e/6a) **Sandsend** (Stage 7d/7e) **Skelton** (Stage 5d/5e) **Staithes** (Stage 6b/7a) **Whitby** (Stage 7e/8)	Arriva X4/X4A
7d/7e Sandsend	**Boulby** (Stage 6b) **Easington** **Hinderwell** (Stage 7a/7b; 0.4 miles OR) **Lythe** (Stage 7c/7d; 1 mile OR) **Middlesborough** **Redcar** **Runswick Bank Top** (Stage 7b/7c) **Saltburn** (Stage 5e/6a) **Skelton** (Stage 5d/5e) **Staithes** (Stage 6b/7a) **Whitby** (Stage 7e/8)	Arriva X4/X4A

Secondary Trail-head	Possible Destinations by Bus (Mainline train stations in red)	Bus/Train Services
7e/8 Whitby	**Boulby** (Stage 6b) **Charltons** (near Slapewath; Stage 5b/5c) **Easington** **Guisborough** **Hinderwell** (Stage 7a/7b; 0.4 miles OR) **Leeds** **Lythe** (Stage 7c/7d; 1 mile OR) **Malton** **Middlesborough** **Pickering** **Redcar** **RHB** (Stage 8/9a) **Runswick Bank Top** (Stage 7b/7c) **Saltburn** (Stage 5e/6a) **Sandsend** (Stage 7d/7e) **Scarborough** (Stage 9d/10a) **Skelton** (Stage 5d/5e) **Staithes** (Stage 6b/7a) **York**	Train services Arriva X4/X4A Arriva X93 Coastliner 840
8/9a RHB	**Charltons** (near Slapewath; Stage 5b/5c) **Guisborough** **Middlesborough** **Scarborough** (Stage 9d/10a) **Whitby** (Stage 7e/8)	Arriva X93
9b/9c Ravenscar	**Burniston** (9d; 1.3 miles OR) **Cloughton** (9d; 1.2 miles OR) **Scarborough** (Stage 9d/10a)	East Yorkshire Buses 115
9d Burniston (1.3 miles OR)	**Cloughton** (9d; 1.2 miles OR) **Ravenscar** (Stage 9b/9c) **Scarborough** (Stage 9d/10a)	East Yorkshire Buses 115
9d Cloughton (1.2 miles OR)	**Burniston** (9d; 1.3 miles OR) **Ravenscar** (Stage 9b/9c) **Scarborough** (Stage 9d/10a)	East Yorkshire Buses 115
9d/10a Scarborough	**Bridlington** **Burniston** (9d; 1.3 miles OR) **Cayton Bay** (Stage 10a/10b) **Cayton** (Stage 10a/10b; 1 mile OR) **Charltons** (near Slapewath; Stage 5b/5c) **Cloughton** (9d; 1.2 miles OR) **Filey** (Stage 10b) **Guisborough** **Helmsley** (Stage 1a) **Leeds** **Malton** **Middlesborough** **Pickering** **Ravenscar** (Stage 9b/9c) **RHB** (Stage 8/9a) **Whitby** (Stage 7e/8) **York**	Train services Arriva X93 Coastliner 843 East Yorkshire Buses 10/12/13/115/128 Shoreline Suncruiser: Filey Flyer 555
10a/10b Cayton Bay/ Cayton (1 mile OR)	**Bridlington** **Filey** (Stage 10b) **Scarborough** (Stage 9d/10a)	East Yorkshire Buses 10/12/13 Shoreline Suncruiser: Filey Flyer 555
10b Filey	**Bridlington** **Cayton Bay** (Stage 10a/10b) **Cayton** (Stage 10a/10b; 1 mile OR) **Scarborough** (Stage 9d/10a)	Train services East Yorkshire Buses 10/12/13 Shoreline Suncruiser: Filey Flyer 555

On the Trail

Ravenscar Radar Station (Stage 9c)

Costs & budgeting

As vacations go, long-distance trekking in the UK is relatively inexpensive. The walking itself is free as no permits are required. The main components of daily expenditure are food and accommodation/camping: approximate costs are set out below.

	Approximate Cost (subject to change)
Room in pub/inn	**£35-75 per person (sharing a double/twin room)**
B&B	**£35-75 per person (sharing a double/twin room)**
Bed in hostel	**£20-30 per person**
Bed in bunkhouse/ camping barn	**£12-30**
Camping	**£5-15 per person**
Meal in pub/inn	**£12-20**
Packed lunch	**£6-10**
Beer (1 pint)	**£4-6**

Weather

Northern England has famously green countryside and this beautiful greenery requires plenty of water. The water is, of course, supplied by rain and England's location near the Atlantic Ocean ensures that there is plenty of it: the island bears the brunt of many Atlantic fronts as they make their way eastwards. Accordingly, there is a fair chance that you will experience rain at some point on the CLW. You might be lucky and walk in perfect conditions but you should always be prepared for wet weather, even in summer. Northern England can also be windy and you should take care on the higher and more exposed parts of the CLW.

In summer, the sun can be strong with temperatures occasionally approaching 30°C. The heat saps your energy and there are long stretches on the moors and cliffs where there is little shade. Hot conditions reduce the distance that you can cover each day: dehydration and sunstroke are possibilities and you should carry more water than normal.

Always obtain a weather forecast before setting out. Many internet sites provide forecasts, with a varying degree of reliability. The UK Met Office (**www.metoffice.gov.uk**) is one of the most reliable as it provides regularly updated localised forecasts for different places along the CLW. It also provides, free of charge, an excellent smart-phone app that displays local forecasts.

Maps

In this book, we have included real maps for the entire CLW: each stage has 1:25,000 scale maps produced by Ordnance Survey, GB's mapping agency. We believe that these are the finest, and most detailed, maps available. They are perfect for navigating the CLW. However, if you would also like sheet maps, there are several options:

- **OS Explorer 1:25,000:** the maps that are printed in this book are based on OS Explorer sheets. Three sheets are required to cover the entire CLW: OL26 (North York Moors: Western area), OL27 (North York Moors: Eastern area) and 301 (Scarborough, Bridlington & Flamborough Head).
- **OS Landranger 1:50,000:** five sheets are required to cover the entire CLW: 100 (Malton & Pickering), 99 (Northallerton & Ripon), 93 (Middlesbrough), 94 (Whitby & Esk Dale) and 101 (Scarborough).
- **Harvey Cleveland Way XT40:** this 1:40,000 waterproof strip map covers the entire trek.

However, perhaps the best overall solution is to combine the real maps provided in this book with OS's excellent smart-phone app: it provides 1:25,000 maps for the whole of GB and uses GPS to show your location and direction on the map. As the app's maps are the same as those provided in this book, they can be used together seamlessly. One month's subscription to the app is only £4.99.

Paths and waymarking

The CLW mainly follows clear paths and tracks which are well maintained. There are also some short sections along minor roads. From time to time, the CLW crosses roads and farm tracks: take care at crossings, looking both ways for traffic.

A typical signpost

In winter, early spring and late autumn, or after sustained periods of rain, some paths can be wet and muddy. However, for much of late spring, summer and early autumn, conditions underfoot are drier.

Much of the countryside is farmland so there are numerous gates and stiles along the way. Like many routes in rural England, the CLW has countless twists and turns as it negotiates rights-of-way through farmland and villages. Fortunately, the route is consistently marked on the ground with clear CLW signs and waymarks. Nevertheless, take care on the moors in low visibility or bad weather when the flat, featureless expanses can be confusing: carry a compass and follow the directions carefully.

On the CLW, there are hundreds of junctions so it is impossible to refer to all of them in the route descriptions. Generally, we only mention junctions if they are particularly significant or if the correct routing is unclear. As a rule of thumb, remain on the main path unless instructed otherwise by signs/waymarks on the ground or the maps/route descriptions in this book: however, keep your wits about you because there will, of course, be the occasional exception to this rule. Also, remember that waymarking is at the mercy of the environment: for example, signs and waymarks are occasionally obscured by vegetation or destroyed by falling trees.

Storing bags

Often walkers from the UK travel to the CLW carrying only the gear that they will actually take on the trek. However, trekkers from further afield, and those who want to spend some time elsewhere after the trek, will probably have additional baggage which they need to store while trekking. Normally, a hotel that you have stayed at near the start of the trek will let you store bags until your return: check when booking. At the end of the trek, it is possible to return to the start by public transport: see 'Travel between Filey and Helmsley'. Alternatively, sometimes businesses that offer baggage transfer are also willing to store surplus luggage: see below.

Baggage transfer

Businesses offering baggage transfer services can transport your bags to your accommodation each night so that you only need to carry a small day-pack on the trail. This spares you from the burden of having to carry a heavy backpack and enables you to pack more clean clothes and some luxuries. Most of the companies offering unguided tours will organise baggage transfers as part of the package. The following businesses offer a baggage transfer service along the entire CLW without the requirement to book an unguided tour:

- **Brigantes:** www.brigantesenglishwalks.com; info@bagmovers.com; 01756 770402
- **Sherpa Van:** www.sherpavan.com; info@sherpavan.com; 01748 826917

Fuel for camping stoves/Outdoor shops

Airlines will not permit the transport of fuel so campers who are flying to the UK will need to source it upon arrival, before setting out on the trek. At the primary trail-heads, Homeworks Hardware Store (Helmsley) and Cammish Outdoors (Filey) stock standard screw-in gas canisters. Along the CLW, there are also outdoor stores in Whitby (Stage 7e/8) and Scarborough (Stage 9d/10a): methylated spirits and standard screw-in gas canisters are normally available but it is wise to call in advance to check.

- **Helmsley:** Helmsley Outdoors (01439 771628); Homeworks Hardware Store (01439 771646)
- **Whitby:** Mountain Warehouse (01947 600655); Goodricks Outdoors (01947 229614)
- **Scarborough:** Millets (01723 333315); Mountain Warehouse (01723 367558); Trespass (01723 355168)
- **Filey:** Cammish Outdoors (01723 513319)

Gas canisters are also usually available in branches of Halfords: there is a Halfords store in Scarborough. You can order online for collection in-shop. If you need petrol or diesel for a multi-fuel stove, there are service stations along the CLW at Helmsley (Stage 1a), Ingleby Arncliffe (Stage 3a; 2.2 miles OR), Skelton (Stage 5d/5e), Hinderwell (Stage 7a/7b; 0.7 miles OR), Whitby (Stage 7e/8), Scarborough (Stage 9d/10a) and Filey (Stage 10b).

Drinking water

Drinking water will be one of your primary considerations each day. Even in Northern England, the sun can be hot: dehydration and sunstroke are always possibilities. Mains water in the UK is usually safe to drink so you can fill up in the morning at your accommodation. However, water is heavy and therefore it is not always possible to start the day carrying all the water that you will need.

Along the way, there are streams where you could, in theory, fill up. In reality, however, the thought of drinking from the streams along the CLW will not appeal to most people: there are numerous sheep and cattle throughout the countryside and farmers in rural England often use pesticides/fertilisers which may find their way into the watercourses. If you do wish to drink from streams, rivers or lakes, then you should ensure that you have dealt with any contaminants using one or more of the methods described below: however, you should research thoroughly the specific product that you are planning to use to understand its effectiveness and the possible risks. Also, bear in mind that the availability of water in smaller streams may vary depending upon the season and the amount of rainfall over previous weeks and months.

Rather than drinking from streams, most trekkers prefer to take advantage of the pubs/cafés along the route: some have outdoor taps that you can use and at others, the staff will normally fill your bottle for free if you ask politely. In fact, licensed premises in England (those that are authorised to serve alcohol) are required by law to provide 'free potable water' to their customers upon request: what a great excuse to stop for a pint! In addition, there are often shops along the way where you can buy water or other drinks: in the introduction to each Section, we list these shops and other places where refreshments are available. It is good practice to start the day with at least 1.5 litres. Plan carefully so that you know where your next fill-up point will be. Furthermore, always check your water levels when you pass a source of water.

Possible contaminants in stream/lake water include visible particulates (which sometimes give water a brown colour), bacteria, viruses, protozoa (for example, giardia) and parasites. There are a variety of possible ways to treat water:

- **Boiling** is the traditional method. A rolling boil of 1min should kill everything in the water. However, it does not remove visible particulates so the boiled water will remain the same colour as when you found it, which can be off-putting. It also uses up a lot of fuel and takes time so is impractical.

- **Filtering** usually removes visible particulates, working miracles by turning coloured water clear. It also normally removes around 99.9% of bacteria, protozoa and parasites. Filters are often cheap and light. It is the quickest method of treatment so it is useful for long-distance routes. However, most filters cannot remove viruses: if you are concerned about viruses then you will need to invest in one of the more expensive filters that remove them or combine filtering with another method (boiling, UV or chemical treatment)..

- **Chemical treatment** can remove bacteria, protozoa, viruses and parasites (each product is different so read the labels carefully). However, there are many disadvantages to chemicals: they do not remove visible particulates so the water will remain the same colour as when you found it; water treated with chemicals usually has a taste; the water usually cannot be drunk immediately as chemicals take time to kill pathogens; and from a health perspective, consuming chemicals may not be good for you.

- **UV treatment** kills bacteria, protozoa, viruses and parasites. However, it does not remove visible particulates so the water will remain the same colour as when you found it: coloured water can be off-putting and the UV treatment is less effective if the water is not completely clear. The most common products are Steripens which are very light.

Perhaps the best single method for the CLW is filtering which turns the water clear and removes almost everything except viruses: although it is possible, you are unlikely to encounter viruses in water along the CLW and some are prepared to drink water which has only been filtered, running a small risk of virus contamination. However, we prefer to combine filtration with UV treatment (using a Steripen): this removes or kills practically everything.

The actual effectiveness of individual products varies and is beyond the scope of this book so do your research beforehand. However, it is worth noting that many products claim to be 99.9% effective indicating that drinking water from wild sources can never be said to be 100% risk free. You will have to weigh up the risks and make up your own mind. You drink the water at your own risk!

	Visible Particulates	Bacteria	Virus	Protozoa	Parasites
Boiling	✗	✓	✓	✓	✓
Filter	✓	✓	Only top of the range filters remove viruses	✓	✓
Chemical Treatment	✗	✓	✓	✓	✓
UV Treatment (such as Steripen)	✗	✓	✓	✓	✓

If, like many, you do decide to drink from natural sources then, as well as treating the water, there are a few rules that you should follow to reduce further any risk:

- Avoid water where there is evidence nearby of animals, especially cows or sheep: carcasses (of dead animals) or faeces can cause contamination
- Do not collect water downstream from buildings or grazing areas
- Preferably drink from moving water. The faster the better
- The bigger the river/stream the better
- Generally the higher the altitude the better

Ticks

As is often the case in Europe, ticks are present in England. They can carry Lyme disease or tick-borne encephalitis so check yourself regularly. Remove ticks with a tick removal tool (making sure that you get all of it out) and then disinfect the area.

Lambing

Between March and May, many ewes along the CLW will be lambing. Trekkers should be particularly careful not to disturb the sheep at this time: do not bring dogs onto land where there are pregnant ewes. If you spot any ewe in distress, or a lamb that appears to have been abandoned, report it to the nearest farmer.

Walking with dogs

Dogs are generally permitted along the route of the CLW. However, they should be kept under proper control and during lambing season, you should respect any diversions that farmers put in place. Some hotels/B&Bs accept dogs but others do not: check in advance. Sensible guidelines for dog-owners are as follows:

- Never let your dog worry or attack farm animals
- Do not take a dog into fields where there are lambs, calves or other young farm animals
- If you enter a field containing farm animals, keep your dog on a short lead or close at heel and keep as far as possible from the animals. Take particular care around lambs, calves or other young farm animals
- If cattle react aggressively and move towards you, keep calm, let go of your dog and take the shortest, safest route out of the field
- Do not take a dog into fields of vegetables or fruit unless there is a clear path and keep your dog on the path
- In areas where there are ground-nesting birds, keep your dog on a short lead or close at heel during the breeding season (usually March-July) to avoid disturbing the birds
- In recreation areas and public places, avoid causing concern to others by keeping your dog close at heel or on a short lead
- Pick up and remove your dog's faeces if it defecates in a public open place

One of the many boundary markers in the NYMNP (Stage 3a)

Equipment

The village of Staithes (Stage 6b/7a)

The long-distance trekker has no influence over challenges like weather and terrain but can control the contents of a pack carried on the trail. Some trekkers carry only a light day-pack, paying for a baggage transfer service to transport the bulk of their gear to their nightly accommodation: see 'Baggage transfer'. Many others, however, elect to carry all their own gear and it is fair to say that a lot of those people set off carrying equipment which is unnecessary or simply too heavy: this can result in injury and/or exhaustion leading to abandonment. If you are intending to carry your own gear, then you should give equipment choice careful consideration: it will be crucial to your enjoyment of the trek and the likelihood of success.

When undertaking any long-distance route, you should be properly equipped for the worst terrain and the worst weather conditions which you could encounter. On the CLW, a key consideration is rain: you might not get any in practice but you should expect it when planning. In late spring, summer and early autumn, you should carry clothing to combat cold, heat, sun and rain. Getting cold and wet in the hills is unpleasant and can be dangerous. Furthermore, even in England, the sun can be strong.

However, the dilemma is that you should also consider weight and avoid carrying anything unnecessary. The heavier your pack, the harder the trek will be. A trekker's base weight is the weight of their pack, excluding food and water. If you are not carrying camping gear and cooking equipment, it is perfectly possible to get by with a base weight of 5-6kg (13lb) or less. If you intend to carry camping equipment then, by investing in some modern lightweight gear, you could start the trek with a base weight of 8-9kg (17lb) or less. Many people are quick to tell you that the lighter the gear, the greater the price but that is not always the case. While it is true that lightweight gear can be expensive, there are also some excellent lightweight products which are great value. Tents, sleeping bags and backpacks are the three heaviest items that you will carry so they offer the biggest opportunities for weight-saving. But do not ignore the smaller items either as the weight can quickly add up. So, if you can afford it, it is sensible to invest some money in gear before you go. The lighter your gear, the more you will enjoy the trek and the better your chance of success. Be ruthless as every ounce counts.

Recommended basic kit

Layering of clothing is the key to warmth: warm air gets trapped between the layers, acting as insulation, and layers can be removed to shed heat. Merino wool or man-made materials are preferable: they wick moisture away from the skin, keeping you warm. Do not wear cotton: it does not dry quickly and gets cold.

Boots/Shoes	Good quality, properly fitting and worn in. Robust soles (such as Vibram) are advisable. For the CLW, trail-running shoes are adequate but many prefer boots with ankle support. Shoes/boots with a waterproof membrane (such as Gore-Tex) are a good idea.	
Socks	2 pairs of good quality, quick-drying walking socks: wash one, wear one. Hand-wash them regularly, helping to avoid blisters. As a luxury, it is nice to have a third pair to wear in the evenings.	
Waterproof jacket and trousers	A waterproof and breathable rain jacket is essential although it might never leave your pack. Waterproof over-trousers are also advisable.	
Base layers	2 T-shirts and underpants of man-made fabrics or merino wool, which wick moisture away from your body: wash one, wear one. As a luxury, it is nice to have a third set to wear in the evenings.	
Fleeces	2 fleeces. Man-made fabrics.	
Shorts/ Trousers	2 pairs of shorts or walking trousers. Convertible trousers are practical as you can remove the legs on warm days. One pair of shorts and one pair of trousers is also a good combination in summer.	
Warm hat	Always carry a warm hat. Even in summer it can be cold, particularly on windy days.	
Gloves	Early or late season trekkers may wish to bring gloves.	
Down jacket	Advisable in spring, autumn and winter when low temperatures are more likely, especially in the evening and early morning.	
Camp shoes	It is nice to have shoes to wear in the evenings. Flip-flops or Crocs are a common choice as they are light. However, if you have comfortable hiking boots/shoes then you might consider not bringing camp shoes to save weight.	
Waterproof pack liner	Most backpacks are not very waterproof. An internal liner will keep your gear dry if it rains. Many trekkers use external pack covers but we do not find them to be very useful: they flap in the wind and in heavy rain, water still finds its way into the pack around the straps (so you need an internal liner anyway).	
Whistle	For emergencies. Many rucksacks have one incorporated into the sternum strap.	
Head-light with spare batteries	You will need a flashlight if you are camping. And it is good practice to carry one for emergencies: it can assist if you get caught out late and enable you to signal to rescuers.	

Basic first-aid kit	Including plasters, a bandage, antiseptic wipes and painkillers. Blister plasters, moleskin padding or tape (such as Leukotape) can be useful to prevent or combat blisters. A tick removal tool or card is also recommended.
Map and compass	For maps, see page 47. A GPS unit or a smart-phone app can be a useful addition but they are no substitute for a map and compass: after all, batteries can run out and electronics can fail.
Knife	Such as a Swiss Army knife. You are going to need to cut that cheese!
Sunglasses, sun hat, sunscreen and lip salve	Even in England, the sun can be strong so do not set out without these items.
Walking poles	These transfer weight from your legs onto your arms, keeping you fresher. They also save your knees (particularly on descents) and can reduce the likelihood of falling or twisting an ankle.
Phone and charger	A smart-phone is a very useful tool on a trek. It can be used for emergencies. Furthermore, apps for weather, mapping and hotel booking are invaluable. It can also replace your camera to save weight.
Towel	If you are staying at campsites or bunkhouses, you will need a towel: lightweight trekking towels are good.
Toiletries	Campers will need to bring soap/shower gel: a small hotel-size bottle should be enough to last the trek, saving a lot of weight. An almost empty toothpaste tube will also save weight. For those who shave, shaving oil is a lightweight alternative to a can of foam/gel. Leave that make-up behind!
Ziplock plastic bag	A lightweight way of keeping money, passport and credit cards dry.
Ear plugs	Useful if staying in dormitories: you will thank us if someone snores!
Emergency food	Carry some emergency food over and above your planned daily rations. Energy bars, nuts and dried fruit are all good.
Water	See 'Drinking water' above. Hydration packs with tubes enable drinking on the move.
Toilet paper and trowel	Bring a backpacking trowel in case nature calls on the trail: bury toilet waste and carry out used toilet paper.
Backpack	Your backpack is one of the heaviest items that you will carry. The difference in the weights of various packs can be surprisingly large. 35 litres should be sufficient if you are not carrying camping gear. 45-60 litres should be adequate for campers. If you need a pack bigger than these then you are most likely carrying too much. Look for well-padded shoulder straps and waist band. Much of the weight of the pack should sit on your hips rather than your shoulders.
Bug repellent	In summer, midges are present so some campers bring bug repellent

Additional gear for campers

Tent: this is one of the heaviest things that you will carry so it provides a big opportunity for weight saving. Some 2-person tents weigh more than 3kg while others weigh less than 0.6kg. The heaviest ones are normally built for extreme winter conditions and are overkill for the normal CLW trekking season. The lightest ones are quite fragile but this is not normally an issue on the CLW where campsites are grassy. Although a few premium brands charge a lot for their products and there are some very expensive tents at the lightest end of the scale, these days there are plenty of lightweight tents available at a reasonable price. Tents weighing 1 to 1.5kg often strike a good balance between price, longevity and weight. Consider money spent here as an investment in your well-being and enjoyment of one of the world's great trails. Believe us when we say that a few kgs can be the difference between success and failure.

Your tent should be waterproof to ensure that you stay dry during rainy nights. If you are going to use a very light tent then a footprint can be a good idea to protect its base: 'footprint' is a trendy, modern word for what used to be known as a groundsheet. Sometimes you can buy footprints specific to your tent model but we prefer to use a sheet of Tyvek which can be cut to size: Tyvek is extremely tough and is cheaper, and normally lighter, than most branded footprints.

Tent pegs: tent weights provided by manufacturers normally exclude the weight of the pegs. The pegs actually provided with tents tend to be quite heavy and many trekkers buy replacement ones which are lighter. Six heavy pegs can weigh as much as 240g while 6 light pegs can weigh as little as 6g. There are many different types available these days and it is important to match the peg with the type of ground they will be used in. The ground on the CLW is soft and normally grassy so it is usually easy to get pegs into it. Accordingly, they do not need to be too strong.

Sleeping bag: each bag has a 'comfort rating': This is the lowest temperature at which the standard woman should enjoy a comfortable night's sleep. There is also a 'lower comfort limit' which is for men. That may sound simple but it is not. Although all reputable sleeping bag manufacturers use the same independent standard, the bags are not tested in the same place so there is a lack of consistency amongst ratings. Also, the ratings are designed with an average man and woman in mind but every person is different: some people get colder than others. The ratings should therefore be used as a guide only and it is wise to choose a bag with a comfort rating which is a few degrees lower than the night temperatures that you will encounter. In June, July and August a bag rated at 5-10°C is normally sufficient. In early and late season, you may want something warmer. However, you do not want to bring a bag that is much too warm as that would add unnecessary weight to your pack.

Unfortunately, with sleeping bags, price tends to be inversely proportional to weight. This is largely because the lightest bags are filled with goose/duck down which is expensive. Synthetic bags are also available but they are much heavier so down is a better choice for trekking. The disadvantage of down bags is that they can lose their warmth if they get wet but that is less likely if you have a good tent and pack liner. Our advice is first to decide what comfort rating you will require. Then choose the lightest bag (with that rating) which you can afford.

Sleeping mat: this makes it comfortable for you to sleep on the hard ground and insulates you from the ground's cold surface. There are three types: air, self-inflating and closed-cell foam. The advantages and disadvantages of each are set out below. For the CLW, weight is normally more of an issue than warmth so we prefer air mats.

Sleeping Mat Type	Pros	Cons
Air mats: need to be blown up	Lightest Very comfortable Most compact when packed Thicker: good for side sleepers	Most expensive Hard work to inflate Can be punctured Less warm than self-inflating
Self-inflating mats: a combination of air and closed-cell foam. The mat partially inflates itself when the valve is opened	Warmest Very comfortable Quite compact More durable than air mats Firmness is adjustable by adding air	Heavier More expensive than closed-cell foam Can be punctured
Closed-cell foam mats	Light Least expensive Most durable Cannot be punctured	Not compact: need to be strapped to the outside of your pack Least warm Least comfortable

Pillow: some use rolled-up clothing but we prefer inflatable trekking pillows which only weigh around 50g.

Stove: you should choose a stove that uses a type of fuel which is available on the CLW. Airlines do not permit you to carry fuel on planes so, if you are flying to England, you will need to source fuel on arrival. Although methylated spirits are sometimes stocked in outdoor shops, these days gas is more widely available (see 'On the Trail'). Most gas stoves are designed to fit generic screw-on canisters (not Campinggaz) which are readily available in the UK. Canisters for Campinggaz stoves (which are popular in France) are much harder to find so are not a good choice for the CLW. Multi-fuel stoves that burn petrol and/or diesel are useful though: the locations of service stations along the CLW are listed on pages 48-49.

Hundreds of different stoves are available, some more complicated than others. Often the lightest ones are the most simple and often the most simple ones are relatively inexpensive. If, like most campers, you will eat dried food such as pasta and rice then your stove will need to do little more than boil water. A basic stove which mounts on top of a gas canister will therefore be adequate: such a stove should also be cheap and lightweight (less than 100g).

Pots: if, like most campers, you eat dried food such as pasta and rice then you will only need one pot which will do little more than boil water. To save weight, go for the smallest pot that you can get away with. For example, if you are travelling solo and planning to use freeze-dried backpacking meals then you would need nothing bigger than a 500-600ml pot. Titanium pots are usually the lightest but they are slightly more expensive. Get the lightest one that you can afford.

Fork/Spoon: we love Sporks! They have a spoon at one end and a fork at the other. They weigh only 9g and cost very little.

Safety

The 'Miner's Bait Table' (Stage 6b)

On a calm summer's day, northern England is paradise. But a sudden weather shift or an injury can change things dramatically so treat the countryside with respect and be conscious of your experience levels and physical capabilities. The following is a non-exhaustive list of recommendations:

- The fitter you are at the start of your trip, the more you will enjoy the hiking.
- Start early to avoid walking during the hottest part of the day and to allow surplus time in case something goes wrong.
- Where possible, do not stray from the waymarked paths so as to avoid getting lost and to help prevent erosion of the landscape.
- Before you set out each day, study the route and make plans based upon the abilities of the weakest member of your party.
- Get a weather forecast (daily if possible) and reassess your plans in light of it. Avoid exposed routes if the weather is uncertain.
- Never be too proud to turn back if you find the going too tough or if the weather deteriorates.
- Bring a map and compass and know how to use them.
- Carry surplus food and clothing for emergencies.
- Avoid exposed high ground in a thunderstorm. If you get caught out in one then drop your walking poles and stay away from trees, overhanging rocks, metal structures and caves. Generally accepted advice is to squat on your pack and keep as low as possible.
- In the event of an accident, move an injured person to a safe place and administer any necessary first-aid. Keep the victim warm. Establish your exact coordinates and, if possible, use your cell-phone to call for help. The emergency number is **999**. If you have no signal then send someone for help.
- When cooking on a camping stove, place the stove on the ground. Avoid using it on a picnic table. We have witnessed a walker knocking over his stove and spilling boiling water on his legs: this is a sure-fire way to end your trek.

General Information

Language: English is the main language.

Charging electronic devices: the UK uses a 3-pin plug. Visitors from outside the UK or Ireland will need an adapter. Some campsites facilitate the charging of electronic devices but this may not be possible at the more basic places. Many people carry portable power packs for charging their devices.

Money: the UK uses Sterling (£). On the CLW itself, there are ATMs in Helmsley (Stage 1a), Skelton (Stage 5d/5e), Saltburn-by-the-Sea (Stage 5e/6a), Whitby (Stage 7e/8), Scarborough (Stage 9d/10a) and Filey (Stage 10b). Credit cards are accepted almost everywhere.

Visas: citizens of the European Union, Australia, New Zealand, Canada or the US do not need a visa for short tourist trips to the UK.

Cell-phones: there is generally good network along the CLW. Occasionally, however, it can be difficult to get a signal. When network is available, it is likely to be a 4G/5G service, enabling access to the internet from smart-phones.

International dialling codes: the country code for the UK is +44. If dialling from overseas, the 0 in UK area codes is omitted.

WiFi: nearly all hotels, pubs and B&Bs have WiFi (see Accommodation Listings). Some campsites do not offer it.

Emergencies and rescue: rescue services are normally free and are provided by unpaid volunteers. The emergency number is **999**: ask for 'mountain rescue'.

Insurance: depending upon your nationality, any required medical treatment in the UK may not be provided free of charge so it is wise to purchase travel insurance which covers hiking.

Tourist Information: there are manned tourist information centres at **Sutton Bank National Park Centre** (Stage 2a; 01845 597426) and **Whitby** (Stage 7e/8; 01723 383636). The following websites are useful too:

- **www.northyorkmoors.org.uk:** the official website for the NYMNP
- **www.yorkshire.com:** the official website of the Yorkshire Tourist Board
- **www.visityorkshire.co.uk:** Yorkshire tourist information
- **www.nationaltrust.org.uk**: this charity owns/manages many sites along/near the CLW
- **www.english-heritage.org.uk**: this charity owns/manages many sites along/near the CLW

Further reading & bibliography:

- **North York Moors & Yorkshire Wolds** by Mike Bagshaw (Bradt; 2023)
- **Stones and Crosses of the North York Moors** by Steve Estill (Fonthill Media; 2017)
- **The Rough Guide to Yorkshire** by Rachel Mills & Olivia Rawes (2021)

Wildlife

A lapwing in flight (Stage 2c)

The CLW is a long trek which crosses a variety of different habitats and many different species of wildlife are present. On the W half of the trek, the moors comprise one of the largest expanses of heather moorland in the world. The E half, on the other hand, is predominately coastal terrain. There is also plenty of woodland and rolling farmland. Land mammals include roe deer, foxes, badgers, rabbits, grey squirrels, hedgehogs, mice, shrews, voles, stoats, weasels and bats. There are also hares which are often confused with rabbits but in fact, they are quite easy to tell apart: hares have distinctive pointy faces and longer ears (with black tips). Some streams and rivers have otters, minks and water voles. As regards reptiles, you may spot an adder, Britain's only venomous snake. Off the coast, there are porpoises and whales (minke, pilot, fin and sei) but they usually prefer the deeper waters further away from the shore. There are also common and grey seals.

There is plenty of interesting birdlife too: listen out for the unmistakeable call of the cuckoos and the tapping of woodpeckers. Also scan the skies for birds of prey such as buzzards, red kites (recognisable by their forked tails), peregrine falcons, merlins and sparrowhawks: they soar high above, searching for prey. If you wish to see some of these fabulous birds close up, then you can visit the National Centre for Birds of Prey (located on the outskirts of Helmsley).

On the moors, you would be unlucky not to see red grouse: well-camouflaged amongst the heather, they take flight as you pass by. Skylarks will keep you company and there are plenty of wading birds too including lapwing (with its distinctive wings and crest), snipe and golden plover. The lovely curlew (with its curved beak and distinctive call) is also present: in winter, they congregate in coastal areas and in summer, return to their inland breeding grounds.

On the coastal sections of the trail, oystercatchers, terns, gannets, guillemots, razorbills, auks, puffins and kittiwakes are all present. In fact, the chalk cliffs around Filey are home to the largest population of sea-birds in the UK.

Plants and Flowers

Foxgloves

The farmland and woodland of the CLW have plenty of wild-flowers, particularly in spring. The bluebells in the woods are a sight to behold in April/May. Gorse is also widespread and its yellow flowers are a dominating feature of the countryside in spring: anyone who walks through a section of bright gorse will be struck by the mouth-watering coconut aroma. In the hedgerows, hawthorn is seemingly everywhere: those who visit in spring, will be treated to an incredible display of hawthorn blossom. Those walking the CLW in late summer and early autumn will find plenty of blackberries. Purple sloe berries (which grow on blackthorn) are common too: they look like giant blueberries but they do not taste like them! In fact, sloe berries are only really palatable when added to gin.

There is plenty of wild heather moorland on the CLW. In fact, it is thought that 75% of the world's heather moorland is found in the UK: it developed over thousands of years, as humans felled woodland to create grazing for livestock. Red grouse feed on the heather which flowers in August, painting the moors a vibrant shade of purple. Many landowners allow grouse shooting which often goes hand in hand with the controversial practice of managed burning of heather: burning destroys the old, woody heather and encourages the growth of new heather shoots which are more palatable to the red grouse. If heather moorland was not managed, it would eventually be lost: scrub and trees would gradually reclaim the land. However, burning raises complex environmental issues such as the possible impact on water quality, wildfire risk and global warming. Other moorland plants include bog cotton, bog asphodel, cloudberry and juniper (some of which are relics of the Ice Age).

Hawthorn Blossom

Surprisingly, woodland and forest cover 23% of the NYMNP: a third of this is broadleaved or mixed woodland; coniferous plantations (predominately created in the 20th century to increase GB's timber stocks after the two world wars) comprise the other two thirds. Common deciduous trees are beech, ash, oak, sycamore, birch, rowan and hazel. Alder thrives along the banks of streams and rivers. Some of the trees are very old and, in fact, ancient woodland (over 400 years old) covers 5% of the NYMNP.

North York Moors National Park

The view from Battersby Moor (Stage 4)

The NYMNP covers 554 square miles of North Yorkshire: 23% is woodland with one of the largest concentrations of ancient trees in England. The park was established in 1952 and contains one of the largest expanses of heather moorland in the world. The moors are divided up by a series of deep valleys (dales) which are home to farms, villages and woodland. The highest point is Urra Moor (454m) which you will cross on Stage 4.

Tourism and agriculture are the key sources of income. Around 8 million people visit the park each year. More than 23,000 people live within the park. The NYMNP contains more than 1400 miles of public rights of way for hikers. A number of long-distance walking routes cross the park including the CLW and Wainwright's Coast to Coast Path (for further information, see our book 'Trekking the Coast to Coast Path').

The NYMNP has more than 1500 ancient boundary stones and crosses including the famous Young Ralph Cross which is the park's emblem. In 2020, the park was named as an International Dark Sky Reserve, recognising its remoteness and low level of light pollution.

1 Helmsley/Kilburn exit

For W-E trekkers, Section 1 is a gentle and pleasant introduction to the trek. Easy paths and tracks climb gradually through woods and farmland before emerging suddenly at a magnificent viewpoint on the edge of the escarpment at Sutton Bank: you will enjoy fabulous views across the Vale of Mowbray. From there, you head S along the rim of the escarpment (Roulston Scar) to the Kilburn White Horse (see p68): allow plenty of time to savour the vistas which are amongst the most memorable on the entire trek. E-W trekkers, on the other hand, will enjoy these far-reaching views early in the stage before a gentle descent to Helmsley. Half a mile from the route of Stage 1a, you will find Rievaulx Abbey (see p71) which is well worth a visit: the café is a good place to take a break.

The town of Helmsley is an excellent place to start/finish the CLW: the official start/finish is at the old Market Cross in Market Place (the town square). As the only market town in the NYMNP, Helmsley has excellent facilities for trekkers: as well as plenty

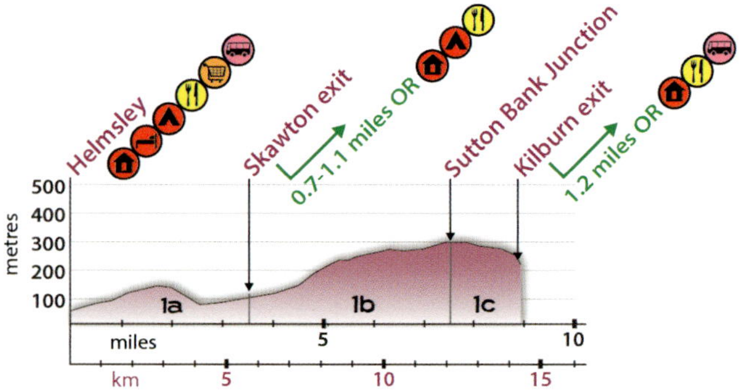

The wonderful view from Roulston Scar (Stage 1c/2a)

of places to stay and eat, there are good shops where you can purchase supplies before setting out on the trail. Helmsley also has some interesting attractions (see p67).

Away from Helmsley, there are not that many accommodation options on Section 1 so book well in advance. At the W end of the section, you can stay in the village of Kilburn which has a pub and a B&B. However, as Kilburn is 1.2 miles OR, many W-E trekkers prefer to continue N along Section 2 to spend their first night at High Paradise Farm: this makes for a long day but avoids the need to descend from the escarpment to search for accommodation. Mid-section, you can stay at the Hare Inn in Scawton (1.1 miles OR) or the nearby Bungdale Head Farm Campsite (0.7 miles OR). There is also camping at Wethercote Farm Campsite (1.4 miles OR).

Section 1 uses clear paths and tracks which are easy to walk upon. There are frequent waymarks, so route-finding is largely straightforward.

		Time	Distance	Ascent W-E	Descent W-E
Stage 1a	Helmsley/ Scawton exit	1:45	3.5miles 5.7km	436ft 133m	256ft 78m
Stage 1b	Scawton exit/ Sutton Bank Junction	2:00(W-E) 1:45(E-W)	4.1miles 6.6km	686ft 209m	92ft 28m
Stage 1c	Sutton Bank Junction/ Kilburn exit	0:30	1.3miles 2.1km	13ft 4m	213ft 65m

Accommodation

- **Helmsley (Stage 1a):** hotels, B&Bs & YHA hostel
- **Scawton (Stage 1a/1b; 1.1 miles OR):** The Hare Inn
- **Kilburn (Stage 1c/2a; 1.2 miles OR):** The Forresters Arms; Church Farm B&B

Camping

- **Helmsley (Stage 1a):** YHA Helmsley
- **Scawton (Stage 1a/1b; 0.7 miles OR):** Bungdale Head Farm Campsite
- **Wethercote Farm Campsite (Stage 1b; 1.4 miles OR)**

The lovely farmland on Section 1 provides a gentle introduction to the trek

Refreshments/Food

- **Helmsley (Stage 1a):** cafés, pubs, restaurants & take-aways
- **Helmsley Walled Gardens (Stage 1a):** Vine House Café
- **Rievaulx Abbey (Stage 1a; 0.5 miles OR):** café
- **Scawton (Stage 1a/1b; 1.1 miles OR):** The Hare Inn
- **Kilburn (Stage 1c/2a; 1.2 miles OR):** The Forresters Arms

Supplies

- **Helmsley (Stage 1a):** supermarket; pharmacy; outdoor store; shops; ATM

Escape/Access

- **Helmsley (Stage 1a):** East Yorkshire Buses 128; Moorsbus M3/M4/M5/M31
- **Rievaulx Abbey (Stage 1a; 0.5 miles OR):** Moorsbus M4
- **Kilburn (Stage 1c/2a; 1.2 miles OR):** North Yorkshire County Council bus no.59

W-E

Stage 1a: Helmsley to Scawton exit

S From the **Market Cross** in **Market Place**, head W. Shortly, TR and walk NW along **Church Street**. Soon, TL onto **Cleveland Way**. Shortly afterwards, at a stone seat (carved with an acorn and many CLW place names), keep SH on a track. Shortly after that, pass the **Vine House Café** at **Helmsley Walled Gardens** (see p67).

1 1:10: TL onto a path alongside **Ingdale Howl**.

2 1:25: At a junction, keep SH across **Rievaulx Bridge**: alternatively, TR before the bridge to visit **Rievaulx Abbey** (0.5 miles OR; see p71).

F 1:45: Reach a junction: for **Stage 1b**, TR and go through a gate, continuing on a track. Alternatively, keep SH for **Scawton** (1.1 miles OR).

E-W

Stage 1a: Scawton exit to Helmsley

F From the junction, head E along the road.

2 0:20: Cross **Rievaulx Bridge**. Immediately afterwards, reach a junction: keep SH for **Stage 1a** or TL to visit **Rievaulx Abbey** (0.5 miles OR; see p71).

1 0:35: TR and head SE on a track. Eventually, shortly after passing the **Vine House Café** at **Helmsley Walled Gardens** (see p67), keep SH at a stone seat (carved with an acorn and many CLW place names). Shortly afterwards, TR along **Church Street**. Soon, TL into **Market Place**.

S 1:45: Arrive at the **Market Cross** in **Helmsley**. Congratulations! You have completed the CLW.

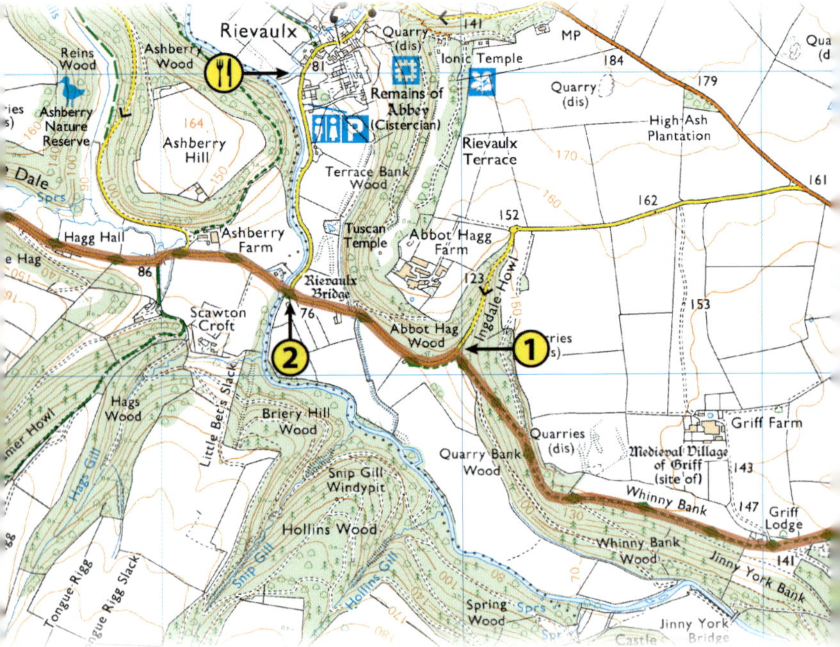

What to see in Helmsley (www.visithelmsley.co.uk)

- **Helmsley Castle** was built in the 12th century by Walter Espec (a.k.a. Walter the Woodpecker) who also founded Rievaulx Abbey. During the English Civil War, it was besieged by Oliver Cromwell's forces for three months until they finally blew up the Great Keep, cutting it in half. The Tudor mansion within the castle walls survived and you can still visit it today along with the remains of the East Tower. The Castle is managed by English Heritage.
- **Helmsley Walled Garden** was built in 1758 to grow fruit for the Feversham family at Duncombe Park. During WW1, most of the gardeners were killed in battle and few returned home to tend the garden. Consequently, after the war, the garden fell into disrepair. In 1994, a local nurse, Alison Ticehurst, had the idea of turning it into a community therapeutic garden space. Sadly, she died before the garden was finished. Today the garden is largely maintained by volunteers. For more information, see **www.helmsleywalledgarden.org.uk**.
- **The National Centre for Birds of Prey** is located on the outskirts of Helmsley in the grounds of Duncombe Park. Its 40 aviaries house the largest collection of birds of prey in the north of England including vultures, eagles, owls, hawks and falcons. They fly the birds for visitors daily. For further information, see **www.ncbp.co.uk**.
- **Helmsley Brewing Co** is a craft brewery located on Bridge Street. It offers brewery tours on Wednesdays. For further information, see **www.helmsleybrewingco.co.uk**.

Helmsley (Stage 1a)

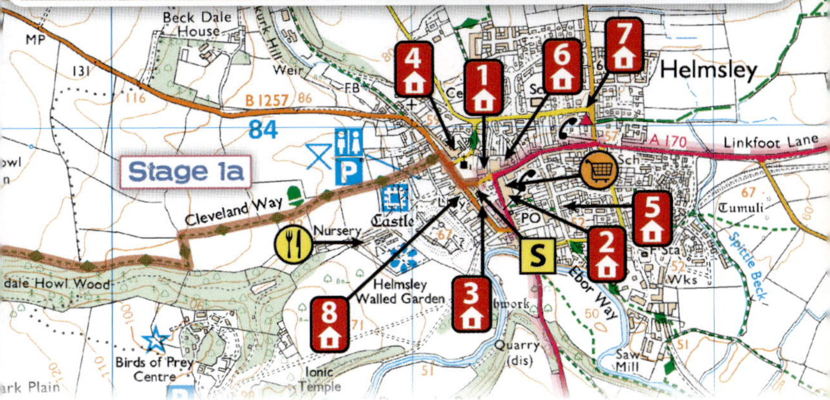

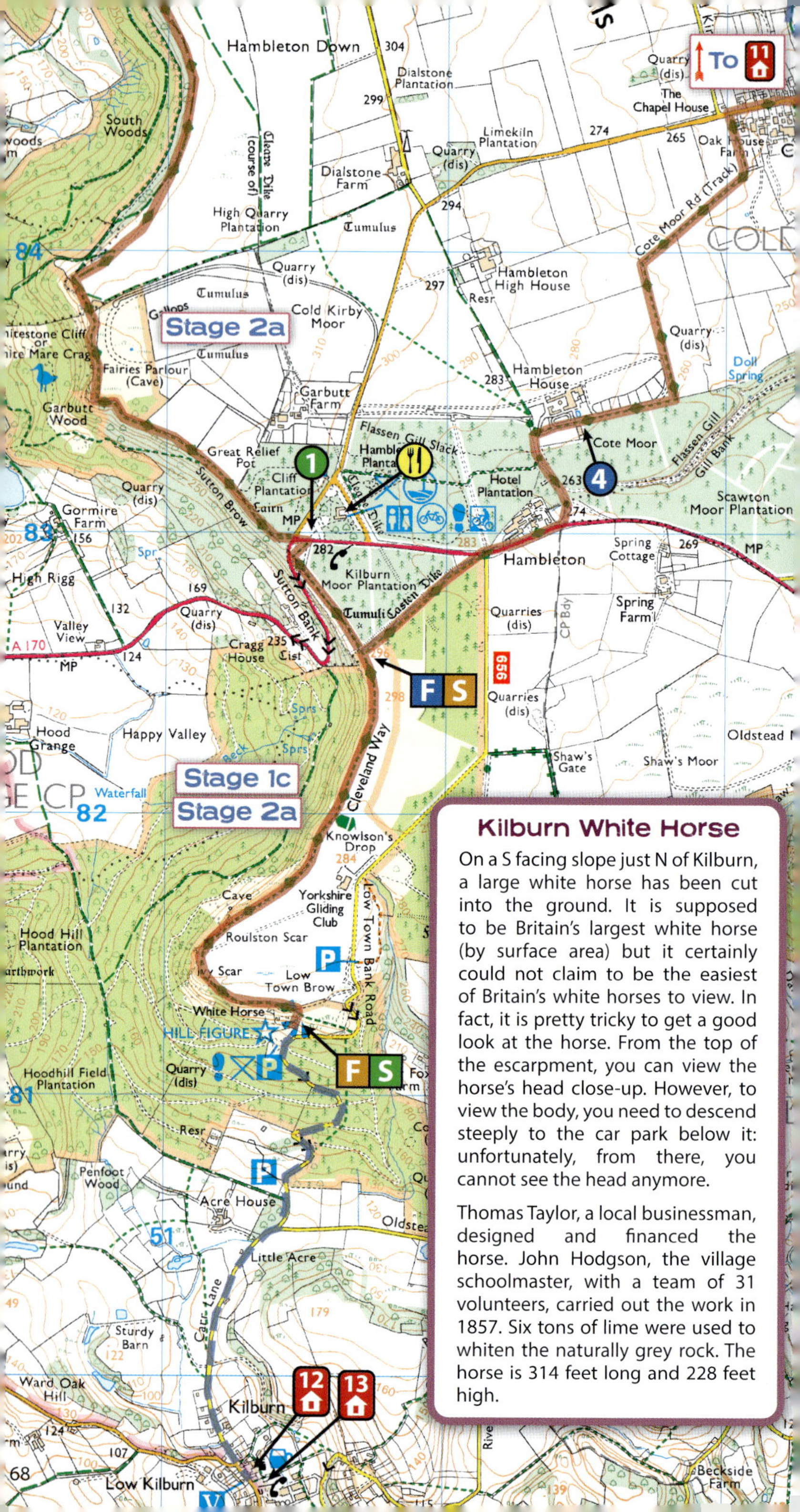

Kilburn White Horse

On a S facing slope just N of Kilburn, a large white horse has been cut into the ground. It is supposed to be Britain's largest white horse (by surface area) but it certainly could not claim to be the easiest of Britain's white horses to view. In fact, it is pretty tricky to get a good look at the horse. From the top of the escarpment, you can view the horse's head close-up. However, to view the body, you need to descend steeply to the car park below it: unfortunately, from there, you cannot see the head anymore.

Thomas Taylor, a local businessman, designed and financed the horse. John Hodgson, the village schoolmaster, with a team of 31 volunteers, carried out the work in 1857. Six tons of lime were used to whiten the naturally grey rock. The horse is 314 feet long and 228 feet high.

W-E

Stage 1b: Scawton exit to Sutton Bank Junction

S From the junction, go through a gate and head initially NW on a track.

1 0:20: TR and cross stepping stones over a stream: alternatively, TL for **Scawton** (0.7 miles OR). Just afterwards, go through a gate. Immediately afterwards, keep SH at a confusing junction, walking W on a track.

2 0:35: TR onto another track. Just afterwards, TR and climb between trees.

3 1:00: TR and descend on a path (easy to miss). 5min later, keep SH at a road in **Cold Kirby**. 5min later, at the far end of the village, TL on a track.

4 1:40: Go through a gate and keep SH along the side of horse gallops. A few minutes later, TL at a junction onto a track. Shortly afterwards, ignore a path on the right (which heads directly to Sutton Bank). A few minutes later, keep SH on a path alongside a road. Soon, cross the road at a junction: then head SW on a path through trees.

F 2:00: Reach a junction: TL to head to the **White Horse/Kildale** along **Stage 1c**. Alternatively, TR to start **Stage 2a** (avoiding the White Horse/Kildale).

E-W

Stage 1b: Sutton Bank Junction to Scawton exit

F From the junction, head NE. 5min later, emerge from trees at a road: cross over and TR alongside it. 5min later, TL on a track. Soon, TR and walk along the side of horse gallops.

4 0:15: Go through a gate and keep SH on a track. At the W side of **Cold Kirby**, TR on a road. 5min later, at the far end of the village, pick up a path climbing E.

3 0:55: A few minutes later, TL on **Low Field Lane**.

2 1:15: TL on a track.

1 1:30: Keep SH at a confusing junction. Immediately afterwards, go through a gate. Just afterwards, cross stepping stones over a stream. Then TL and head E on a track: alternatively, head S for **Scawton** (0.7 miles OR).

S 1:45: Reach a junction: TL for **Stage 1a** or TR for **Scawton** (1.1 miles OR).

W-E

Stage 1c: Sutton Bank junction to Kilburn exit

S Head S from the junction on a superb balcony path: there are plenty of benches where you can rest while enjoying the excellent views W across the Vale of Mowbray. Eventually, the path passes along the top of the **Kilburn White Horse** (see p68) although you cannot see much of it from here. Soon, you can descend steps to the car park below the horse: from there, you can see most of the horse (but sadly, not its head!).

F 0:30: From the car park, retrace your steps for **Stage 2a**: alternatively, you can descend S along the road to **Kilburn** (1.2 miles OR).

E-W

Stage 1c: Kilburn exit to Sutton Bank junction

F From the car park, climb back up the steps. Then head N along the escarpment.

S 0:30: Reach the junction previously passed on Stage 2a.

The beautiful deciduous woodland on Stage 1a

Rievaulx Abbey (0.5 miles OR)

Rievaulx was an abbey of the Cistercian order and was founded in 1132. By 1167, the abbey housed 140 monks and 500 lay brothers. In the 14th century, the Black Death hit the community hard and the Abbey's population had decreased to 23 by the time it closed in 1538 (during King Henry VIII's dissolution of the monasteries). The King sold it to Thomas Manners, 1st earl of Rutland, who dismantled many buildings. Rutland also took advantage of the abbey's water-powered forge to establish an ironworks: by 1545, it had four furnaces. In the 1640s, the ironworks closed because the local timber, which was used to heat the furnaces, had been exhausted. Afterwards, the Duncombe family bought the property.

During the 1750s, in an attempt to make the site more aesthetically pleasing, Thomas Duncombe built a terrace above the abbey with classical temples at either end. After that, the abbey became popular with visitors including artists and writers. However, by the start of the 20th century, the ruins were close to collapse. In 1917, they were taken over by the Office of Works and repairs were commenced.

Today the abbey is managed by English Heritage. You can wander amongst the ruins and there is a visitor centre, museum and café. For more information, see **www.english-heritage.org.uk**.

2 Kilburn exit/Osmotherley

Section 2 can be divided into two halves with High Paradise Farm as the centre point. The S half follows the edge of a steep-sided escarpment (lying just inside the W borders of the NYMNP): it provides magnificent views to the W over the Vale of Mowbray and the Vale of York. You will pass Sutton Bank which was a favourite place of local author, James Herriot. In fact, he famously declared that the view from Sutton Bank was the finest in England: you may agree or disagree with this statement but it is irrefutable that the vista is spectacular on a fine day. The Sutton Bank National Park Centre is only a short distance from the trail: it is a great source of information on the region and has a café and shop.

The N half of Section 2 is completely different, leading you across moors for the first or last time (depending upon your direction of travel). This vast expanse of grass and heather is perched high above the Vale of Mowbray to the W so the fine views continue (although you will have to peer over the beautifully maintained

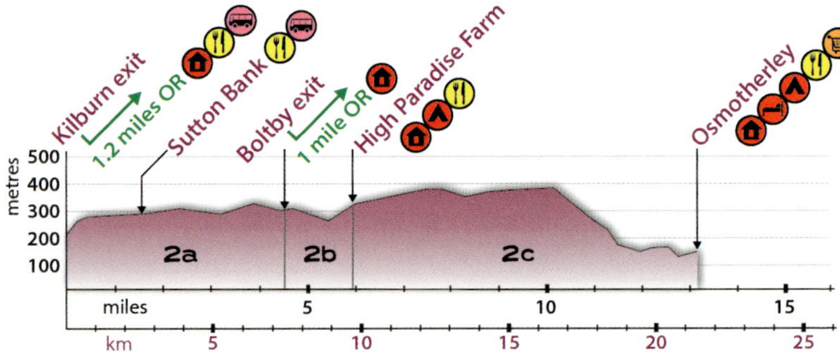

View from the moorland escarpment on Stage 2c

dry-stone walls to enjoy them). The walking here is delightfully easy and, if you are lucky, you will be accompanied by the unmistakable cries of the many lapwings which visit this area: there are curlew, grouse and partridge too.

For W-E trekkers, Section 2 finishes at Osmotherley which is one of the loveliest overnight stops on the CLW. Within the village, there are two pubs and a hotel which all offer food, accommodation and great beer. Those on a budget will be pleased to find a youth hostel and a campsite (N of the village centre). E-W trekkers will finish Section 2 at the Kilburn White Horse which has been cut into the slopes of Roulston Scar (see p68): the village of Kilburn (which has a pub and a B&B) is 1.2 miles OR from there.

High Paradise Farm (in the middle of Section 2) is a popular option with rooms and a campsite: book in advance. You can also stay at Willow Tree Cottage B&B at Boltby (Stage 2a/2b; 1 mile OR).

Section 2 uses clear paths and tracks which are easy to walk upon. There are frequent waymarks, so route-finding is largely straightforward.

		Time	Distance	Ascent W-E	Descent W-E
Stage 2a	Kilburn exit/ Boltby exit	2:00(W-E) 1:45(E-W)	4.5miles 7.3km	397ft 121m	180ft 55m
Stage 2b	Boltby exit/ High Paradise Farm	0:45	1.4miles 2.3km	207ft 63m	144ft 44m
Stage 2c	High Paradise Farm/Osmotherley	3:15(W-E) 3:30(E-W)	7.3miles 11.7km	489ft 149m	1014ft 309m

Accommodation

- **Kilburn (Stage 1c/2a; 1.2 miles OR):** The Forresters Arms; Church Farm B&B
- **Boltby (Stage 2a/2b; 1 mile OR):** Willow Tree Cottage B&B
- **High Paradise Farm (Stage 2b/2c)**
- **Osmotherley (Stage 2c/3a):** Queen Catherine Hotel; The Golden Lion; The Three Tuns; Vane House B&B; Cote Ghyll Mill Youth Hostel (0.3 miles OR)

Camping

- **Wethercote Farm Campsite (Stage 2a; 1.1 miles OR)**
- **High Paradise Farm (Stage 2b/2c)**
- **Osmotherley (Stage 2c/3a):** Cote Ghyll Caravan & Camping Park (0.3 miles OR)

Refreshments/Food

- **Kilburn (Stage 1c/2a; 1.2 miles OR):** The Forresters Arms
- **Sutton Bank National Park Centre (Stage 2a):** Park Lite Café
- **High Paradise Farm (Stage 2b/2c):** café offers meals during the day; breakfast hampers & evening meals must be booked in advance
- **Osmotherley (Stage 2c/3a):** Queen Catherine Hotel; The Golden Lion; The Three Tuns; Osmotherley Tea & Coffee Shop; Osmotherley Fish & Chip Shop

Supplies

- **Osmotherley (Stage 2c/3a):** Top Shop Village Store (basic groceries/ sandwiches/snacks/drinks); shop at Cote Ghyll Caravan & Camping Park (basic groceries/drinks; 0.3 miles OR)

Escape/Access

- **Kilburn (Stage 1c/2a; 1.2 miles OR):** North Yorkshire County Council no.59
- **Sutton Bank National Park Centre (Stage 2a):** Moorsbus M4
- **Osmotherley (Stage 2c/3a; 1 mile OR):** Coatham Coaches 80/89

The 'loveliest view in England' can be moody! (Stage 2a)

W-E

Stage 2a: Kilburn exit to Boltby exit

S From the **White Horse car park**, retrace your steps N along the escarpment. At the junction at S, keep SH, heading NW along **Sutton Bank**.

1 0:40: Just after a viewpoint with benches, reach a road. Cross the road and then TL on a path: alternatively, TR for **Sutton Bank National Park Centre**. Shortly afterwards, pass the place that James Herriot called 'the finest view in England': from there, the path contours along the edge of the escarpment.

F 2:00: Reach a junction at **High Barn**: for **Boltby**, TL onto a path which descends steeply W. Alternatively, keep SH for **Stage 2b**. If you miss this junction, you can also reach **Boltby** by descending on the road crossed at **Sneck Yate** (15min further N along Stage 2b).

Stage 2b: Boltby exit to High Paradise Farm

S From the junction, continue N.

1 0:15: Go through a gate just before a forest. Immediately afterwards, TL at a fork, descending on a broad path. Shortly afterwards, keep SH across a road into the forest: the road heads SW to **Boltby**.

2 0:30: Go through a gate. Then keep SH on a lane.

F 0:40: Arrive at **High Paradise Farm**.

E-W

Stage 2b: High Paradise Farm to Boltby exit

F From High Paradise Farm, head S on a lane.

2 0:10: Go through a gate. Then keep SH on a path.

1 0:25: Leave the forest and keep SH across a road (which heads SW to **Boltby**). Shortly afterwards, go through a gate and continue S.

S 0:40: Reach a junction at **High Barn**: for **Boltby**, TR on a path which descends steeply W. Alternatively, for **Stage 2a**, keep SH along the escarpment.

Stage 2a: Boltby exit to Kilburn exit

F From the junction, continue S along the escarpment. Eventually, keep SH past the place that James Herriot called 'the finest view in England'. Shortly afterwards, keep SH along a road, heading E.

1 1:10: TR on a path, heading SW: alternatively, keep SH for **Sutton Bank National Park Centre**. Soon, pass a viewpoint with benches. At the edge of the escarpment, TL and head SE. At the junction at S, keep SH, heading S: alternatively, TL to continue directly to **Helmsley** on **Stage 1b** (without visiting the Kilburn White Horse). Head towards **Roulston Scar** on a superb balcony path: there are plenty of benches so that you can rest while enjoying the excellent views W across the Vale of Mowbray. Eventually, the path passes just above the **Kilburn White Horse** (see p68) although you cannot see much of it from here. Soon, you can descend steps to the car park below the horse: from there, you can see most of it (but sadly, not its head!).

S 1:45: From the car park, retrace your steps for **Stage 1c**: alternatively, you can descend S along the road to **Kilburn** (1.2 miles OR).

Red legged Partridge (Stage 2c)

View from Sutton Bank (Stage 2a)

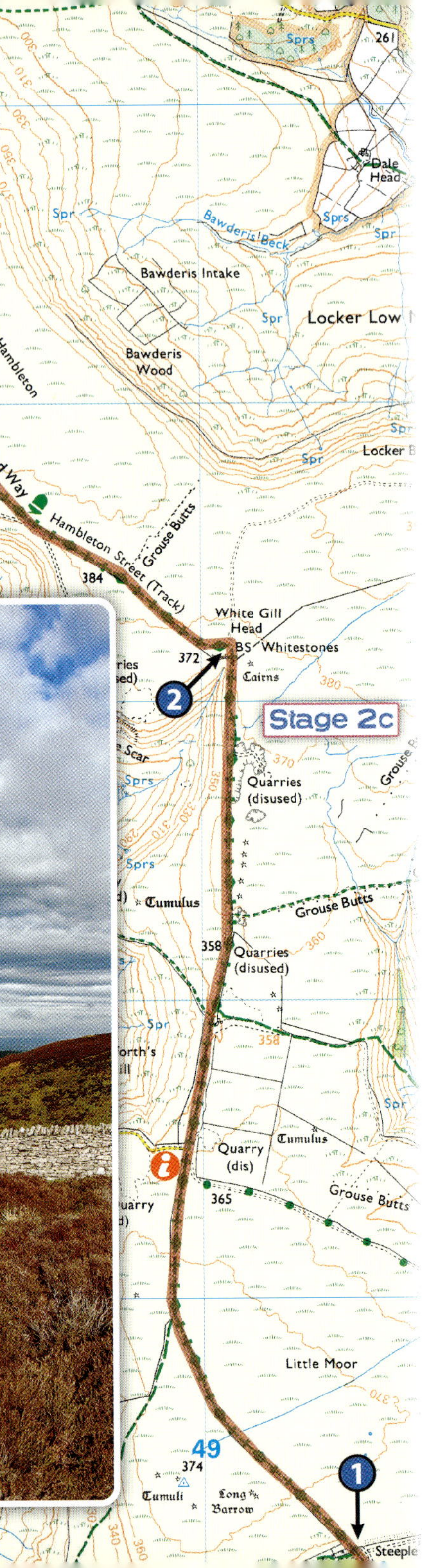

The moors S of Osmotherley (Stage 2c)

W-E

Stage 2c: High Paradise Farm to Osmotherley

S Head NE on a track. A few minutes later, go through a gate. Immediately afterwards, TL at a junction onto a path.

1 0:30: Keep SH through a gate onto **Little Moor** (the first section of moorland on the CLW). Follow a track alongside a wall: this is a great area for spotting lapwings and curlews.

2 1:25: At **White Gill Head**, TL at a fork, remaining close to the wall (which now heads NW).

3 2:20: At the road at **Square Corner**, TL onto a path.

4 2:40: At a junction, keep SH.

5 2:50: TL down a road. Shortly afterwards, TR and climb on a track. A few minutes later, TL on a path which joins a grassy track. After a few minutes, TR on a path.

6 3:05: Keep SH across a track. Immediately after crossing a bridge, TR and climb. Keep SH across a road. Then follow waymarks through alleyways.

F 3:15: Shortly afterwards, arrive in the centre of **Osmotherley**.

E-W

Stage 2c: Osmotherley to High Paradise Farm

F From **Osmotherley**, head E, following waymarks through alleyways. Soon, keep SH across a road.

6 0:10: After crossing a bridge, keep SH across a track. 5-10min later, TR down a track. A few minutes later, TL along a road.

5 0:25: Shortly afterwards, TR and head SE.

4 0:35: At a junction, keep SH, continuing SE.

3 1:00: TR at the road at **Square Corner**, heading S.

2 2:05: At **White Gill Head**, TR and follow a wall S: this is a great area for spotting lapwings and curlews.

1 3:00: Go through a gate and continue SE. 25min later, TR and go through a gate: head SW on a track.

S 3:30: Arrive at **High Paradise Farm**.

Osmotherley (Stage 2c/3a)

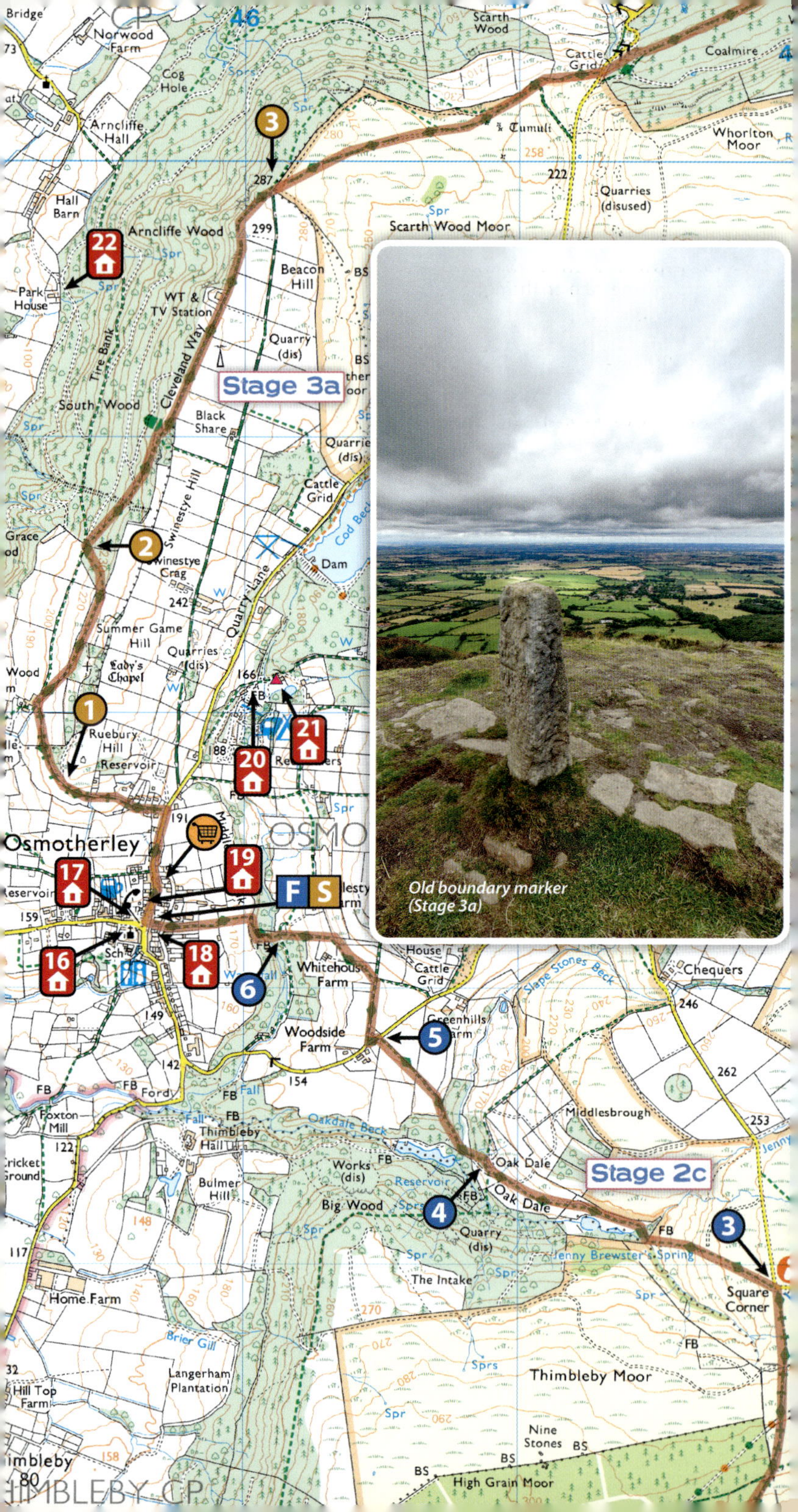

Old boundary marker (Stage 3a)

W-E

Stage 3a: Osmotherley to Lordstones

S From the centre of **Osmotherley**, head N up **North End**. Soon pass the village store. A few minutes later, TL up **Ruebury Lane**.

1 0:15: Keep SH at a fork. 5-10min later, reach a junction where there are two gates: go through the gate on the right and climb on a grassy track.

2 0:35: TR through a gate. Just afterwards, TR at a junction: this is where Wainwright's famous **Coast to Coast Path** joins the CLW. Head N: keep on the main path as you climb, ignoring smaller offshoots.

3 1:05: Head NE at a junction onto **Scarth Wood Moor**. 15min later, TL and descend on a path. 5min later, TL down a road. Shortly afterwards, TR on a path.

4 1:40: TL on a track. Just afterwards, TR on a path. Soon start the long climb to **Carlton Bank**.

5 3:45: Pass the trig point at **Carlton Bank**. Then descend steeply NE. Cross a road and continue on a path.

F 4:00: Shortly afterwards, reach **Lordstones**.

E-W

Stage 3a: Lordstones to Osmotherley

F From **Lordstones**, head SW. Soon cross **Raisdale Road**. Then climb steeply SW.

5 0:20: Pass the trig point at **Carlton Bank**. Then descend S.

4 2:00: TL on a track. Just afterwards, TR and climb SW. Later, TL up a road. Shortly afterwards, TR and continue climbing.

3 3:00: Head SW at a junction.

2 3:20: Keep SH at a junction: this is where the **Coast to Coast Path** leaves the CLW. 5-10min later, go through a gate and head S.

1 3:35: Keep SH at a junction and head E along **Ruebury Lane**. TR down **North End**. Soon pass the village store.

S 3:45: Shortly afterwards, reach the centre of **Osmotherley**.

Typical CLW signpost (Stage 3a)

3 Osmotherley/ Great Broughton exit

Crossing a remote and wild part of the North York Moors, Section 3 is a highlight of the CLW. The path undulates along the N escarpment of the Cleveland Hills, traversing a series of pristine moorland plateaus. To the N, the terrain drops away dramatically, providing glorious uninterrupted views. The scenery is particularly fine in late summer when the heather is in full bloom, painting the hillsides a vibrant shade of purple. You have a good chance of spotting some red grouse and keep your eyes peeled for the old boundary markers along the way. There is also a Bronze Age burial mound beside the path which dates from 2000 BCE.

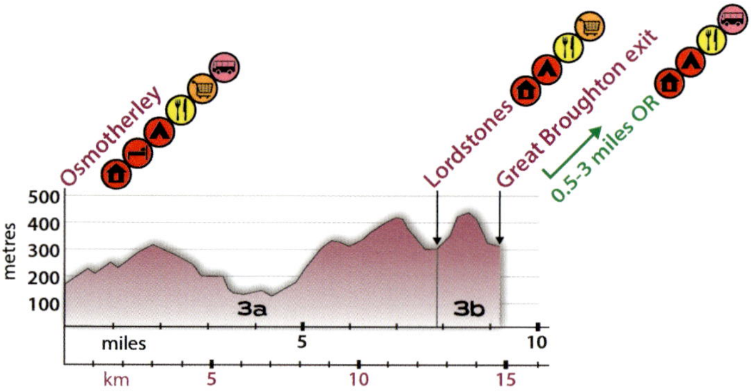

Big views from the moorland plateaus (Stage 3a)

Away from Osmotherley, there are not that many accommodation options on Section 3 so book well in advance. At the E end of the section, you can stay in Great Broughton (2 miles OR; pub/B&Bs) or at Beak Hills Farm (0.5 miles OR; B&B/camping). However, as both are situated OR, some W-E trekkers prefer to overnight at Lordstones which is located mid-section (campsite/camping pods/shop/restaurant/café). Alternatively, if you are in good shape, you could continue along Section 4 to Kildale to spend the night (although this makes for a very long day).

With significant altitude gain/loss, Section 3 is fairly challenging. The terrain is undulating, alternately climbing onto the high moors and then descending towards the lower ground again. Fortunately, the paths and tracks are clear and easy to walk upon, although they can be muddy. The route is well marked, however, moors can be confusing places in low visibility or bad weather: carry a compass and follow the directions carefully.

		Time	Distance	Ascent W-E	Descent W-E
Stage 3a	Osmotherley/ Lordstones	4:00(W-E) 3:45(E-W)	7.8miles 12.5km	1647ft 502m	1211ft 369m
Stage 3b	Lordstones/ Great Broughton exit	0:45	1.5miles 2.4km	476ft 145m	394ft 120m

Scarth Wood Moor (Stage 3a)

Accommodation

- **Osmotherley (Stage 2c/3a):** Queen Catherine Hotel; The Golden Lion; The Three Tuns; Vane House B&B; Cote Ghyll Mill Youth Hostel (0.4 miles OR)
- **Park House Country Guest House (Stage 3a; 0.6 miles OR)**
- **Lordstones (Stage 3a/3b):** camping pods
- **Beak Hills Farm (Stage 3b/4; 0.5 miles OR)**
- **Great Broughton (Stage 3b/4; 2-3 miles OR):** The Wainstones Hotel; Newlands House B&B; Dromonby Bridge B&B

Camping

- **Osmotherley (Stage 2c/3a):** Cote Ghyll Caravan & Camping Park (0.3 miles OR)
- **Lordstones (Stage 3a/3b)**
- **Beak Hills Farm (Stage 3b/4; 0.5 miles OR)**

Refreshments/Food

- **Osmotherley (Stage 2c/3a):** Queen Catherine Hotel; The Golden Lion; The Three Tuns; Osmotherley Tea & Coffee Shop; Osmotherley Fish & Chip Shop
- **Lordstones (Stage 3a/3b):** café, restaurant & bar
- **Great Broughton (Stage 3b/4; 2 miles OR):** pubs

Supplies

- **Osmotherley (Stage 2c/3a):** Top Shop Village Store (basic groceries/sandwiches/snacks/drinks); shop at Cote Ghyll Caravan & Camping Park (basic groceries/drinks; 0.3 miles OR)
- **Lordstones (Stage 3a/3b):** shop (basic groceries/snacks/drinks/legendary pies); water tap beside shop

Escape/Access

- **Osmotherley (Stage 2c/3a; 1 mile OR):** Coatham Coaches 80/89
- **Great Broughton (Stage 3b/4; 2 miles OR):** Moorsbus M4; Coatham Coaches 89

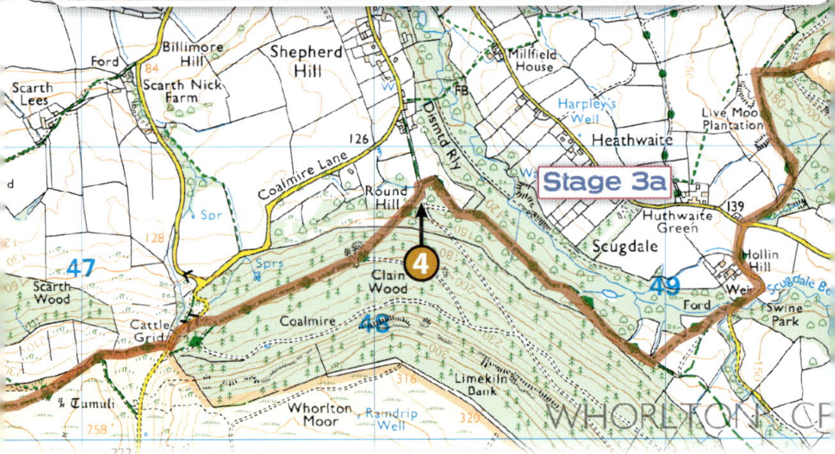

The cafe at Lordstones (Stage 3a/3b)

For Stage 3a descriptions, see p81

The path across Urra Moor (Stage 4)

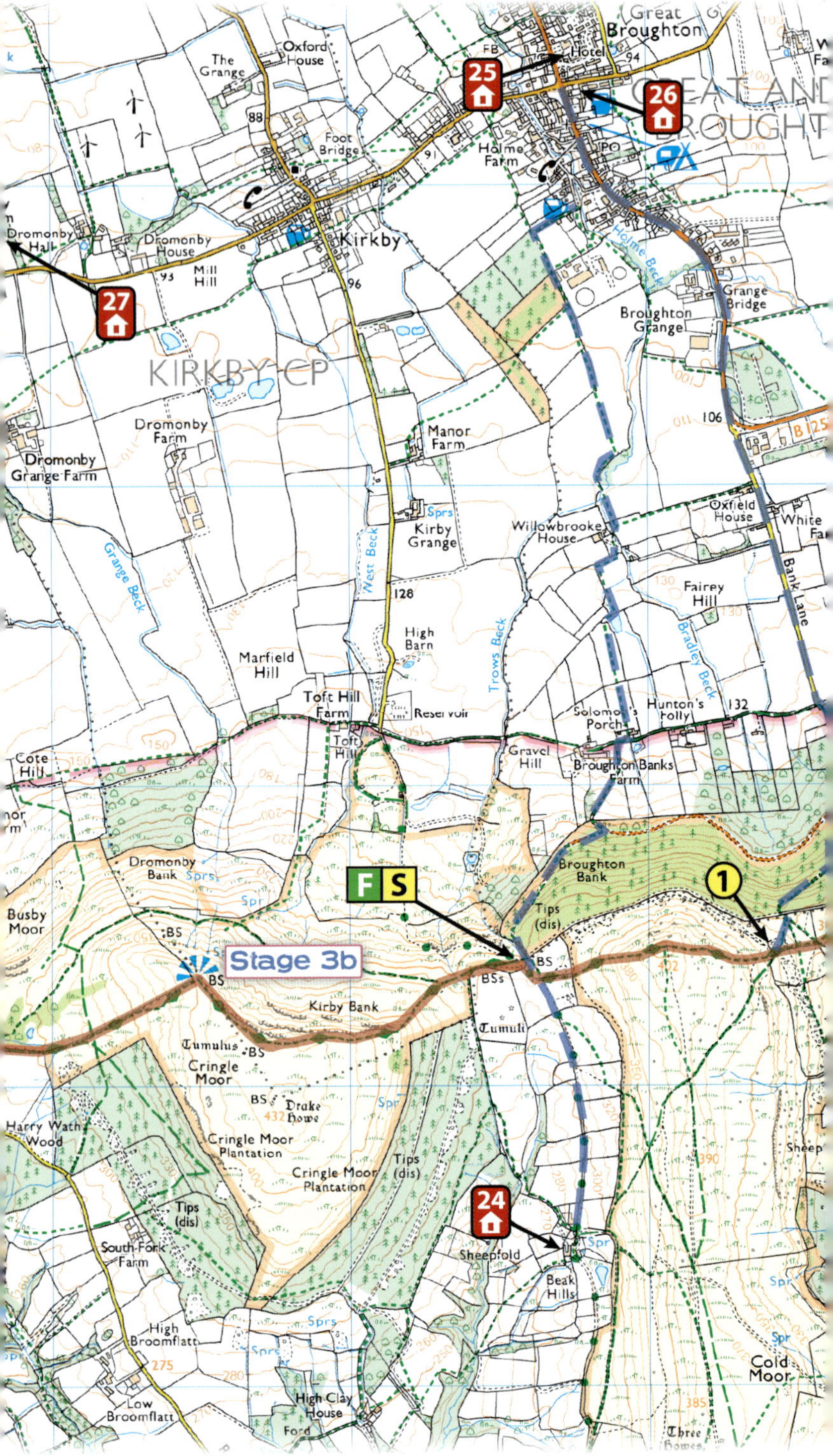

Great Broughton
Hotel
FB
94
25
26
GREAT AND BROUGHTON
Oxford House
The Grange
88
Foot Bridge
91
Holme Farm
PO
Kirkby
Dromonby Hall
Dromonby House
93
Mill Hill
96
27
Holme Beck
Grange Bridge
Broughton Grange
KIRKBY CP
Dromonby Farm
Manor Farm
106
B 1257
Dromonby Grange Farm
Sprs
Kirby Grange
Oxfield House
White Fa
Willowbrooke House
Grange Beck
West Beck
128
Fairey Hill
Bank Lane
Bradley Beck
High Barn
Trows Beck
Marfield Hill
Toft Hill Farm
Reservoir
Solomon's Porch
Hunton's Folly
132
Toft Hill
Gravel Hill
Broughton Banks Farm
Cote Hill
150
Dromonby Bank
Sprs
Spr
Broughton Bank
1
F S
Busby Moor
Tips (dis)
BS
Stage 3b
BSs
402
Kirby Bank
Tumuli
Tumulus
Cringle Moor
Drake Howe
432
Harry Wath Wood
Cringle Moor Plantation
Cringle Moor Plantation
Tips (dis)
Sheep
390
Tips (dis)
24
South Fork Farm
Sheepfold
Spr
Beak Hills
High Broomflatt
275
Sprs
280
Cold Moor
Low Broomflatt
High Clay House
Ford
385
Three Howes

W-E

Stage 3b: Lordstones to Great Broughton exit

S From **Lordstones**, head E and soon climb. TR at a superb viewpoint and walk along **Kirby Bank**. Then descend E.

F 0:45: Reach a fork: TR for **Stage 4** or TL for **Great Broughton**. Shortly afterwards, reach a junction: TR for **Stage 4** or TL for **Great Broughton**. Shortly after that, a path on the right heads S to **Beak Hills Farm**.

E-W

Stage 3b: Great Broughton exit to Lordstones

F Head W and soon climb. Walk W along **Kirby Bank**. TL at a superb viewpoint and then descend W.

S 0:45: Arrive at **Lordstones**.

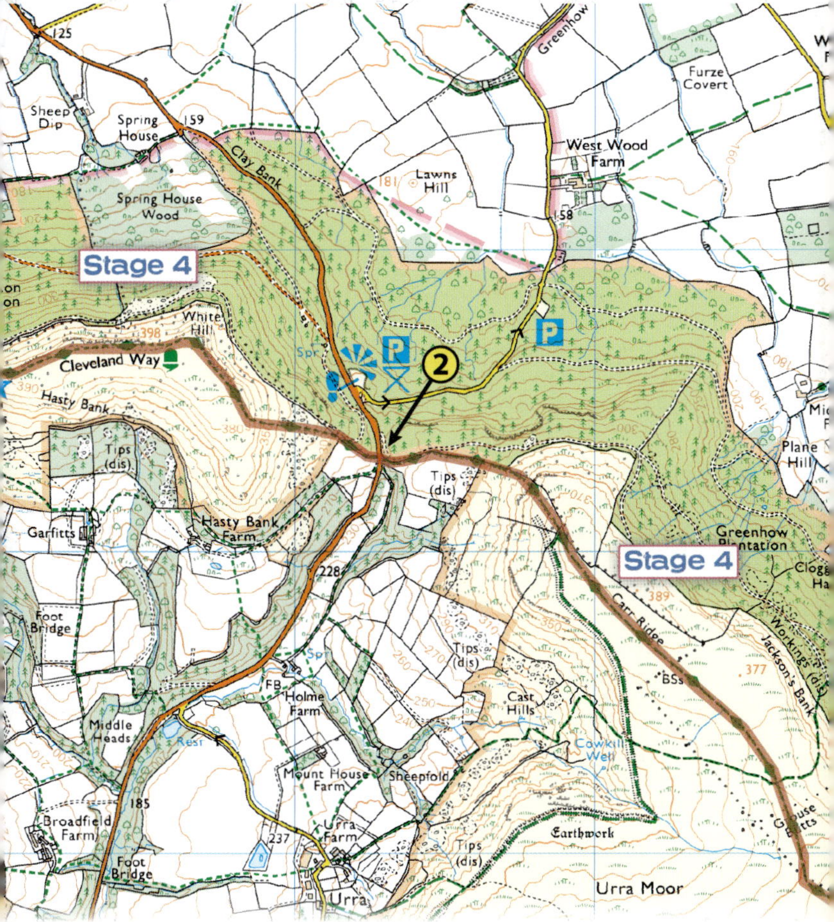

4 Great Broughton exit/ Kildale

Leading you deeper into the North York Moors, Section 4 is the most remote part of the CLW. Between the Great Broughton exit and Clay Bank Top (2), the undulating route heads across the magnificent Hasty Bank and past the Wainstones, a distinctive rocky outcrop which offers one of the most memorable panoramas on the entire trek: on a fine day, this is a wonderful picnic spot. Apparently, there are Bronze Age carvings on some of the rocks of the Wainstones but we wish you luck with finding them!

E of Clay Bank Top, you traverse the wilds of Urra, Ingleby and Battersby Moors and cross Round Hill, the highest point in the NYMNP. Far above the region's roads and settlements, this is a peaceful place and there is a good chance of spotting red grouse. However, if the weather takes a turn for the worse, this high ground is very exposed and you are a long way from shelter. The scenery is particularly fine in late summer when the heather is in full bloom.

Unfortunately, there is not much accommodation alongside the route of Section 4 and there is nowhere at all to stay mid-section. At the stage's N end, you will find

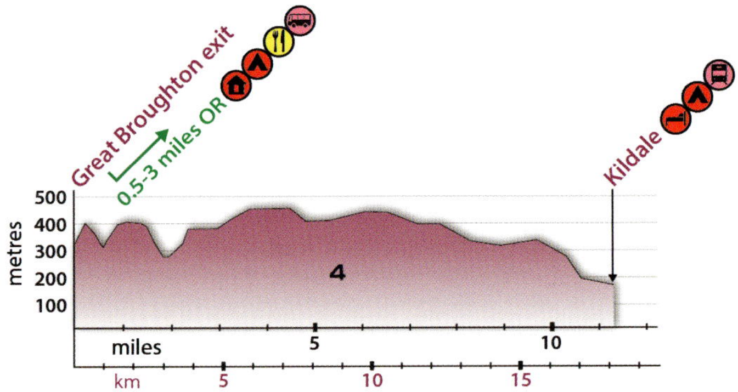

Kildale where many of the cottages were built to house miners who worked in local jet, iron ore and whinstone mines. However, the only surviving accommodation near this lovely village is Kildale Camping & Barn (just SW of the village): the bunk rooms may be too basic for some trekkers. Furthermore, because there is nowhere to buy an evening meal in Kildale, you will need to bring your own food if you want to spend the night. As a result, many trekkers do not stop at Kildale, preferring to hike between Lordstones/Great Broughton and Newton-under-Roseberry/Slapewath in one very long day.

At the W end of the section, you can stay in Great Broughton (2 miles OR; pub/B&Bs) or at Beak Hills Farm (0.5 miles OR; B&B/camping): however, as both are located OR, many E-W trekkers continue past the Great Broughton exit, preferring to overnight at Lordstones which is 45min further W along Stage 3b (campsite/camping pods/ shop/restaurant/café).

W of Clay Bank Top (**2**), the undulating terrain is quite tiring. W-E trekkers get this out of the way early and then have to endure a tough climb to Round Hill: however, after that, the route largely descends gently all the way to Kildale. Section 4 is slightly tougher for E-W trekkers who start with a long climb out of Kildale and, towards the end of the stage, are faced with the tiring undulations W of Clay Bank Top.

Paths and tracks are clear and easy to walk upon, although they can be muddy. The route is well marked, however, moors can be confusing places in low visibility or bad weather: carry a compass and follow the directions carefully.

		Time	Distance	Ascent W-E	Descent W-E
Stage 4	Great Broughton exit/ Kildale	5:45(W-E) 6:00(E-W)	11.3miles 18.2km	1476ft 450m	1962ft 598m

Accommodation

- **Beak Hills Farm (Stage 3b/4; 0.5 miles OR)**
- **Great Broughton (Stage 3b/4; 2-3 miles OR):** The Wainstones Hotel; Newlands House B&B; Dromonby Bridge B&B
- **Kildale (Stage 4/5a):** Kildale Camping & Barn (bunk room accommodation)

Camping

- **Beak Hills Farm (Stage 3b/4; 0.5 miles OR)**
- **Kildale (Stage 4/5a):** Kildale Camping & Barn

Refreshments/Food

- **Great Broughton (Stage 3b/4; 2 miles OR):** pubs
- **Kildale (Stage 4/5a):** Glebe Cottage Tearoom only opens a few days a week, closing at 16:30. Accordingly, it cannot be relied upon and does not offer evening meals

Supplies

- **None**

Escape/Access

- Great Broughton (Stage 3b/4; 2 miles OR): Moorsbus M4; Coatham Coaches 89
- Clay Bank Top (Stage 4): Moorsbus M4
- Kildale (Stage 4/5a): train station

The N escarpment of the Cleveland Hills (Stage 4)

The Handstone and the Face Stone

On Stage 4, near Round Hill, there are two interesting four-sided stone markers. The most westerly of the two markers, the Hand Stone, is thought to have been erected in the 18th century as a navigational aid for travellers crossing Urra Moor. It sits close to the trig point on Round Hill and it had a pair of hands carved on it, although they are now almost indistinguishable. The more easterly marker, known as the Face Stone, gets its name from the human face which was carved on it: this too has been damaged by weathering. There is more uncertainty over the origins of the Face Stone: it seems clear that it pre-dates the Hand Stone (as it was mentioned in 1642 in documents relating to Duncombe Estate), however, some people believe that it dates back to the Iron Age.

Jenny Bradley Cross (4)

Along an old drovers' road on Stage 4, about 1km N of Bloworth Crossing, lie the remains of an ancient moorland cross, known as the Jenny Bradley Cross. The base and part of the upright shaft are all that remain and they are dwarfed by the 18th century boundary marker next to them. There are numerous stone crosses in the North York Moors: some were memorials but others, like the Jenny Bradley Cross, marked boundaries or served as waymarkers. There is little available information on the origin of the cross's name.

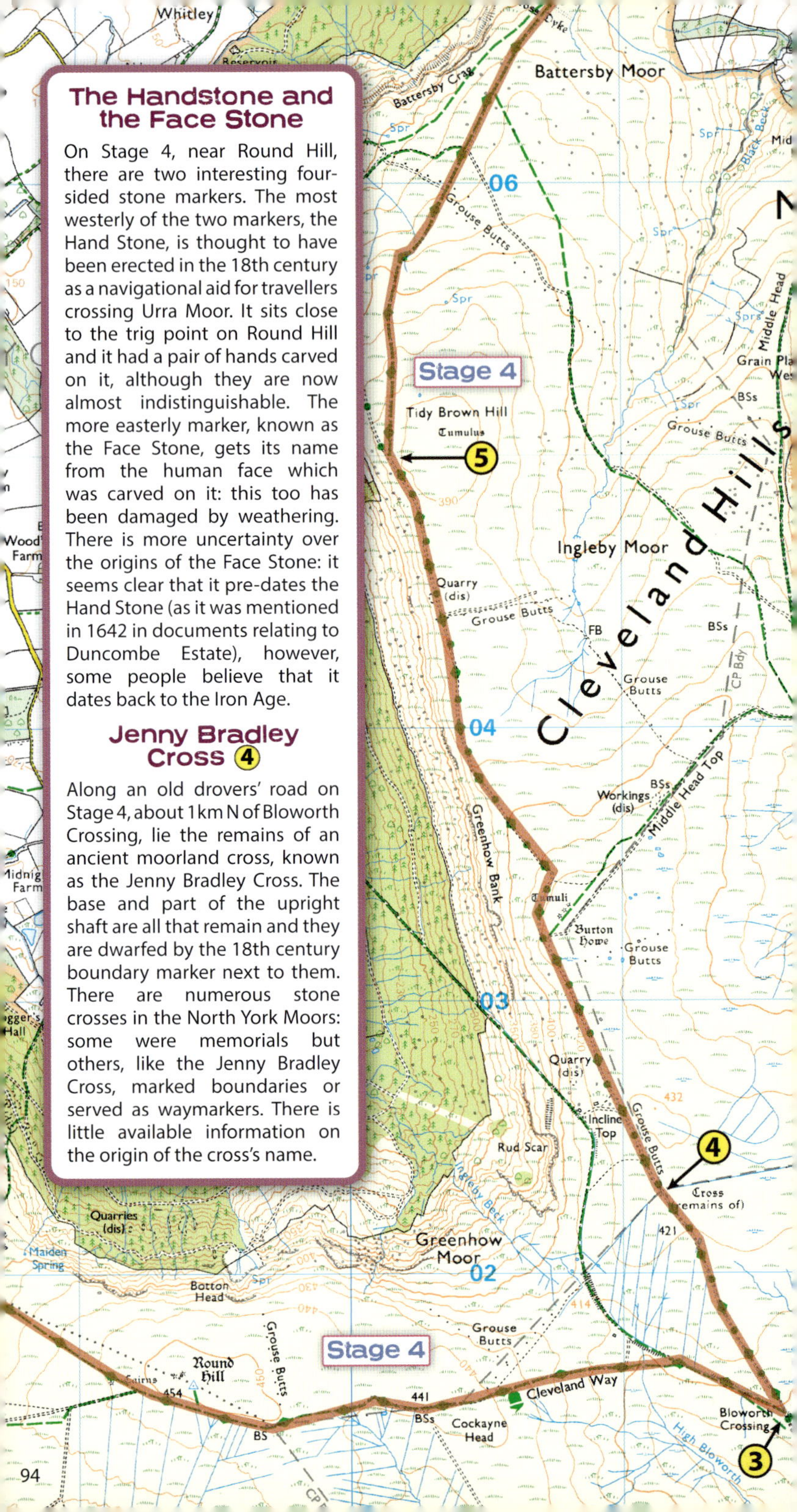

Burton Howe Round Barrow

This Bronze Age burial mound is located a stone's throw from Stage 4 (between 4 and 5). The mound is 1.7m high and it has an 18th century boundary marker on top. It has a diameter of 15m. The mound was excavated in the 1950s but little was found except bone fragments, pieces of an urn and a clay bead.

Rosedale Railway

The 12-mile Rosedale Railway was built to transport ironstone from the remote mines at Rosedale (E of Blakey Ridge) to the blast furnaces of Teesside. It was completed in 1865. By 1929, the mines had closed due to pressure from overseas competition and a decline in the quality of the ore. The railway was ripped up for salvage.

W-E

Stage 4: Great Broughton exit to Kildale

S Climb E across **Cold Moor**. Cross the top of a hill and descend again.

1 0:20: From the bottom of the slope, continue E: the paths on the left lead to **Great Broughton**. Soon climb directly towards a rocky outcrop (**the Wainstones**): take care climbing up through the rocks to the top (superb views). Continue E along the crest of the ridge. Soon descend again.

2 1:00: Cross the road at **Clay Bank Top**. Then climb E. Soon the path bends right, climbing SE over **Urra Moor**. Pass the trig point on **Round Hill (454m)**, the highest point on the CLW. Close by, you will find the '**Handstone**' (see p94). Continue E and soon pass the '**Face Stone**' (see p94).

3 2:40: At **Bloworth Crossing**, TL and head N on a track (leaving the Coast to Coast Path which continues E along the line of the **old Rosedale Railway** (see p95)).

4 2:55 Pass the remains of the **Jenny Bradley Cross** (see p94) and an 18th century boundary marker. About 20min later, pass **Burton Howe Round Barrow** on the right (see p95).

5 3:55: TR at a junction (easy to miss). Descend NE across **Battersby Moor**.

6 4:40: Keep SH along a lane. Follow the lane when it bends left.

7 5:10: Pass a WW2 **memorial** to the crew of a Hudson aircraft which crashed nearby in 1941: there is a similar memorial for a different aircraft on Stage 5a.

8 5:40: TR along a road.

F 5:45: Arrive in the village of **Kildale**.

E-W

Stage 4: Kildale to Great Broughton exit

F From **Kildale**, head SW on the road.

8 0:05: TL and climb on another road.

7 0:40: Pass a WW2 **memorial** to the crew of a Hudson aircraft which crashed nearby: there is a similar memorial for a different aircraft on Stage 5a.

6 1:15: Keep SH and climb SW on a path across **Battersby Moor**.

5 2:05: Keep SH at a junction, heading S.

4 3:10: Pass the remains of the **Jenny Bradley Cross** (see p94) and an 18th century boundary marker.

3 3:25: TR at **Bloworth Crossing**, heading initially NW on a broad path. You now share the route with Wainwright's famous **Coast to Coast Path** which arrives at Bloworth Crossing from the E along the line of the **old Rosedale Railway** (see p95). After a while, continue W past the '**Face Stone**' (see p94). Later, pass the trig point on **Round Hill (454m)**, the highest point on the CLW. Nearby you will find the '**Handstone**' (see p94). Descend NW across **Urra Moor**.

2 5:00: Cross the road at **Clay Bank Top**. Then climb NW onto **Hasty Bank**. From the crest of the ridge, head NW. Soon head W towards a rocky outcrop (**the Wainstones**): take care descending W through the rocks to the right of the outcrop.

1 5:40: From the bottom of the slope, climb W: the paths on the right lead to **Great Broughton**. Cross a hill and descend W.

S 6:00: A path on the left heads S to **Beak Hills Farm**. Just afterwards, reach a junction: TL for **Stage 3b** or TR for **Great Broughton**.

The Wainstones (Stage 4)

5 Kildale/ Saltburn-by-the-Sea

Everything changes over the course of this long stretch of the CLW. For W-E trekkers, there is one last section of moorland to enjoy (between Kildale and Slapewath) before making a dash for the coast across forest and farmland. Your arrival at the Victorian seaside resort of Saltburn-by-the-Sea feels significant: your journey of many days through the mysterious and starkly beautiful moors is over and, for the remainder of the trek, you will follow the line of the spectacular coast. E-W trekkers, on the other hand, will leave the coastline behind and aim for moorland where an entirely new experience awaits.

Stages 5a and 5b are Section 5's most dramatic parts with more of the undulating moorland terrain experienced on Sections 3 and 4. The highlight is the climb of Roseberry Topping, the Matterhorn of Yorkshire, which is an official side route of the CLW: the views are wonderful (see p104). However, if you do not have the energy to head for the summit, you can still enjoy fantastic views of it from the main route.

Saltburn-by-the-Sea is an enjoyable place to stop for the night. There are a handful of places to stay and plenty of restaurants, pubs and cafés. With shops, bakeries and a supermarket, it also provides a good opportunity for resupply. Saltburn-by-the-Sea was a 19th century creation. Originally, 'Old Saltburn' was a small hamlet below the cliffs: its remote location ensured that it was popular with smugglers. Development began when ironstone was discovered nearby. In 1859, Henry Pease,

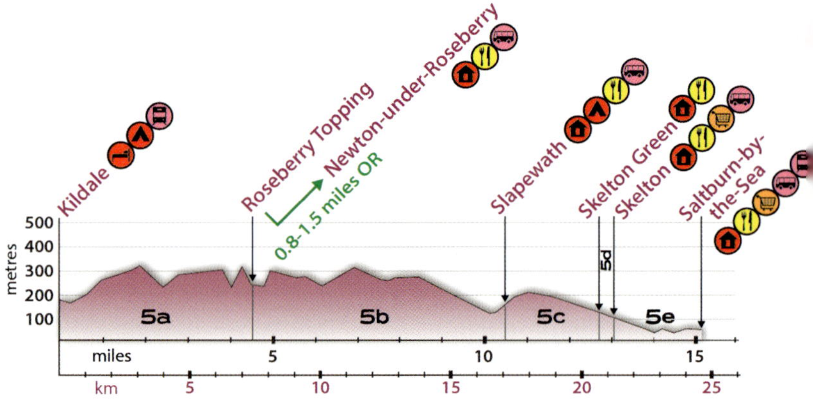

The pier at Saltburn (Stage 5e/6a)

a local entrepreneur, began to implement his ambitious vision for a new seaside resort. He bought land from locals and within 20 years, most of the town had been completed. After Pease died, few new facilities were added and as a result, the town was metaphorically frozen in the Victorian age. For information on Saltburn's famous pier, see p106.

Away from Saltburn, there are not that many accommodation options on Section 5 so book well in advance: Newton-under-Roseberry (Stage 5a/5b; 0.8-1.5 miles OR) has a pub and a hotel; Slapewath has the Fox & Hound Hotel (which is popular with CLW hikers) and you can camp nearby at Margrove Park (0.7 miles OR); Skelton Green has a B&B; Skelton has a hotel.

At the stage's S end, E-W trekkers can stay at Kildale Camping & Barn (just SW of the village of Kildale): for further information on Kildale, see p91.

Paths and tracks are clear and easy to walk upon, although Stages 5a and 5b can be muddy. The route is generally well marked except that on Stage 5b, waymarking is poor E of 2. Furthermore, moors can be confusing places in low visibility or bad weather: carry a compass and follow the directions carefully. At the time of writing, the Stage 5e route through Skelton had changed slightly due to new housing development: we describe the altered route but it is not yet clear if this is a permanent change.

		Time	Distance	Ascent W-E	Descent W-E
Stage 5a	Kildale/ Roseberry Topping	2:15(W-E) 2:00(E-W)	4.5miles 7.2km	1073ft 327m	581ft 177m
Stage 5b	Roseberry Topping/ Slapewath	2:45(W-E) 3:15(E-W)	6.0miles 9.6km	666ft 203m	1322ft 403m
Stage 5c	Slapewath/ Skelton Green	1:00	2.2miles 3.5km	331ft 101m	223ft 68m
Stage 5d	Skelton Green/ Skelton	0:15	0.4miles 0.6km	0ft 0m	157ft 48m
Stage 5e	Skelton/Saltburn-by-the-Sea	1:00	2.2miles 3.5km	141ft 43m	351ft 107m

Accommodation

- **Kildale (Stage 4/5a):** Kildale Camping & Barn (bunk room accommodation)
- **Newton-under-Roseberry (Stage 5a/5b):** King's Head Inn (0.8 miles OR); Pinchinthorpe Hall (1.5 miles OR)
- **Slapewath (Stage 5b/5c):** Fox & Hound Hotel
- **Skelton Green (Stage 5c/5d):** Westerlands Guest House
- **Skelton (Stage 5d/5e):** Wharton Arms Hotel
- **Saltburn-by-the-Sea (Stage 5e/6a):** hotels; B&B; guest house

Camping

- **Kildale (Stage 4/5a):** Kildale Camping & Barn
- **Slapewath (Stage 5b/5c):** Margrove Park (0.7 miles OR)

Refreshments/Food

- **Kildale (Stage 4/5a):** Glebe Cottage Tearoom only opens a few days a week, closing at 16:30. Accordingly, it cannot be relied upon and does not offer evening meals
- **Newton-under-Roseberry (Stage 5a/5b):** King's Head Inn (0.8 miles OR); Pinchinthorpe Hall (1.5 miles OR)
- **Slapewath (Stage 5b/5c):** Fox & Hound Hotel (advance reservation recommended); The Chase Coffee Lounge & Café
- **Skelton Green (Stage 5c/5d):** Miners Arms; Café Creations; London Pizzeria

- **Skelton (Stage 5d/5e):** R&R Bistro; cafés; take-aways
- **Saltburn-by-the-Sea (Stage 5e/6a):** pubs, restaurants, cafés; take-aways

Supplies

- **Skelton (Stage 5d/5e):** supermarkets; pharmacy; ATM
- **Saltburn-by-the-Sea (Stage 5e/6a):** supermarket; pharmacy; shops; ATMs

Escape/Access

- **Kildale (Stage 4/5a):** train station
- **Newton-under-Roseberry (Stage 5a/5b; 0.8 miles OR):** Coatham Coaches 18
- **Charltons (near Slapewath; Stage 5b/5c):** Arriva X93
- **Skelton (Stage 5d/5e):** Arriva 3/X3/X3A/X4/X4A/5/5A
- **Saltburn-by-the-Sea (Stage 5e/6a):** train station; Arriva 3/X3/X3A/X4/X4A; Moorsbus M4

Saltburn Viaduct (Stage 5e)

W-E

Stage 5a: Kildale to Roseberry Topping (Newton-under-Roseberry exit)

S Head NW on **Station Road**. Shortly afterwards, TR onto another road, heading N.

1 0:30: TL up a track. 5min later, TL at a junction onto a path.

2 1:00: TR at **Captain Cook's Monument** (see p103) and descend N on a path. Shortly afterwards, pass a WW2 **memorial** to the crew of a Hudson aircraft which crashed nearby in 1940: Stage 4 has a similar memorial for a different aircraft.

3 1:15: TR along a lane. Shortly afterwards, TL and climb steps.

4 1:50: Reach a junction. Keep SH through a gate to continue on **Stage 5a** (to climb Roseberry Topping): alternatively, TR to head directly to **Slapewath** on Stage 5b (avoiding Roseberry Topping). Descend to a saddle. Then climb a clear path heading up the slope of **Roseberry Topping**.

F 2:15: Arrive on the summit of **Roseberry Topping (320m)**. For **Stage 5b**, retrace your steps E back to **4**: alternatively, to head to **Newton-under-Roseberry**, take one of the paths descending W from the summit: when you meet **Roseberry Lane**, head W to the **A173**.

E-W

Stage 5a: Roseberry Topping (Newton-under-Roseberry exit) to Kildale

F From the summit, retrace your steps E.

4 0:25: TR and head SE on a path. Eventually, descend steps and TR along a lane.

3 0:55: Shortly afterwards, TL and climb on a path. Eventually, pass a WW2 **memorial** to the crew of a Hudson aircraft which crashed nearby in 1940: there is a similar memorial for a different aircraft on Stage 4.

2 1:15: Shortly afterwards, TL at **Captain Cook's Monument** (see p103) and descend E on a path.

1 1:40: TR and head S on a lane.

S 2:00: TL on **Station Road** and arrive in **Kildale**.

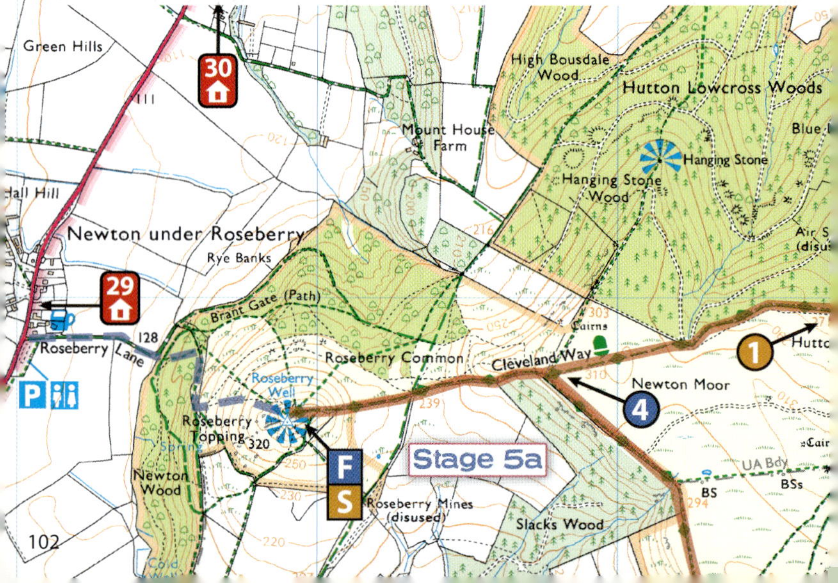

Captain Cook's Monument ②

Captain Cook's Monument was built in 1827 on Easby Moor by Robert Campion, a banker from Whitby. It is a memorial to Captain James Cook, the famous British mariner and explorer, who lived nearby as a child.

Cook was born in 1728. In 1746, he became the apprentice to John Walker (a Whitby ship owner) and quickly learnt to navigate at sea. In 1755, he joined the Royal Navy where he learned how to survey coastlines. In 1763-66, he charted the coast of Newfoundland. In 1768, he led an Admiralty/Royal Society expedition to Tahiti on HMS Endeavour to observe the transit of Venus across the face of the sun. After charting Tahiti, he set out to search for land in the Pacific. He charted New Zealand's coast and the E coast of Australia which he named 'New South Wales'. This opened the door for British colonisation of Australia and parts of the Pacific.

In 1772, Cook embarked on his second great voyage: the Admiralty sent him back to the Pacific to search for the Great Southern Continent which was thought to encircle the South Pole. By circumnavigating the globe further S than anyone before him, he proved that this continent did not exist (unless it was very close to the pole).

In 1776, the Admiralty sent Cook to the Pacific for a third time to search for the Northwest Passage which it was hoped would link the Pacific to the North Atlantic. He explored the W coast of North America but did not find the passage. In 1779, Cook was stabbed to death by islanders in Hawaii.

Cook's three Pacific voyages contributed greatly to European knowledge. He discovered many new lands and charted a great deal of the region. Cook's charts were so accurate that some of them were still used by sailors in the 1950s.

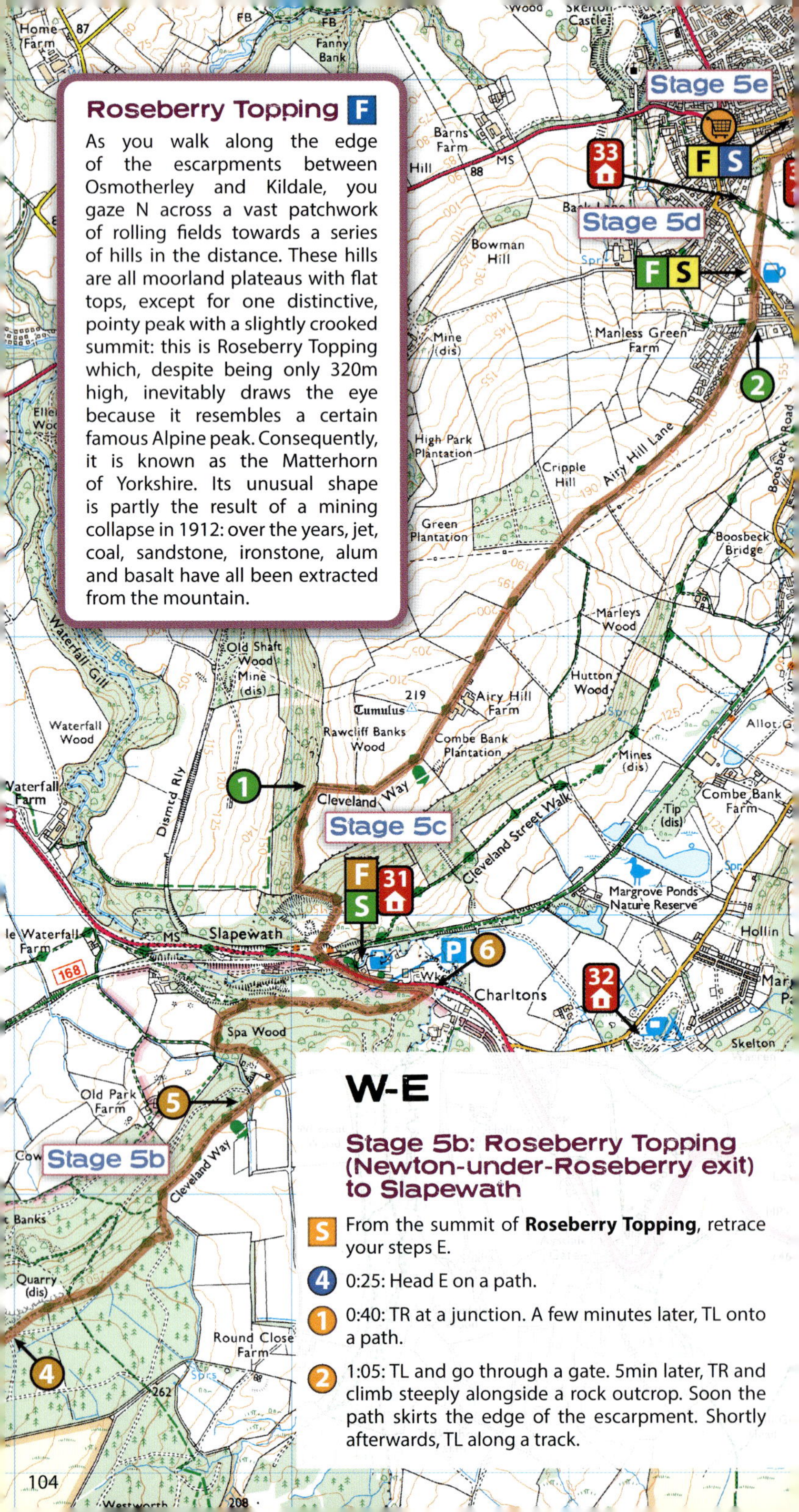

Roseberry Topping F

As you walk along the edge of the escarpments between Osmotherley and Kildale, you gaze N across a vast patchwork of rolling fields towards a series of hills in the distance. These hills are all moorland plateaus with flat tops, except for one distinctive, pointy peak with a slightly crooked summit: this is Roseberry Topping which, despite being only 320m high, inevitably draws the eye because it resembles a certain famous Alpine peak. Consequently, it is known as the Matterhorn of Yorkshire. Its unusual shape is partly the result of a mining collapse in 1912: over the years, jet, coal, sandstone, ironstone, alum and basalt have all been extracted from the mountain.

W-E

Stage 5b: Roseberry Topping (Newton-under-Roseberry exit) to Slapewath

S From the summit of **Roseberry Topping**, retrace your steps E.

4 0:25: Head E on a path.

1 0:40: TR at a junction. A few minutes later, TL onto a path.

2 1:05: TL and go through a gate. 5min later, TR and climb steeply alongside a rock outcrop. Soon the path skirts the edge of the escarpment. Shortly afterwards, TL along a track.

3 1:40: TL at a fork onto a grassy track. A few minutes later, TR at a junction, climbing on a path. A few minutes after that, keep SH on a track. Shortly afterwards, keep SH at a junction. Waymarking is poor in this area.

4 2:00: TL onto a path. A few minutes later, TR at a fork (easy to miss).

5 2:20: TR at a junction. Shortly afterwards, TL down a lane. A few minutes later, TR on a path. Now follow waymarks and signs carefully as there are plenty of twists and turns.

6 2:40: Go through a gate and TL. Keep SH beside a road.

F 2:45: Shortly afterwards, cross the road and reach the **Fox and Hound Hotel** in **Slapewath**.

Stage 5c: Slapewath to Skelton Green

S From the **Fox & Hound Hotel**, head W up a small road. Soon pick up a path alongside a fence. As you climb steeply, remain on the main path, ignoring offshoots.

1 0:20: TR at a junction, continuing alongside a field.

2 0:55: Keep SH on a road.

F 1:00: Reach a junction on the main road at **Skelton Green**.

E-W

Stage 5c: Skelton Green to Slapewath

F Head S on **Airy Hill Lane**.

2 A few minutes later, keep SH at a junction, heading SW on a path.

1 0:45: TL on a path and soon descend steeply. Eventually, head E on a small road.

S 1:00: Reach the **Fox and Hound Hotel** in **Slapewath**.

Stage 5b: Slapewath to Roseberry Topping (Newton-under-Roseberry exit)

F From the **Fox & Hound Hotel**, cross the A171 and head E on a path alongside it.

6 0:05: TR and go through a gate. Head W on a path through **Spa Wood**: follow waymarks and signs carefully as there are plenty of twists and turns. 10min later, TL up a lane. A few minutes later, TR at a junction.

5 0:30: Keep SH at a junction and climb SW. Remain on the main path, ignoring offshoots. After 10-15min, TR at a junction. 5-10min later, TR at a fork. Shortly afterwards, keep SH at a junction. Waymarking is poor in this area.

4 1:00: Keep SH at another junction, continuing SW. After 15-20min, TR (leaving the track) and descend on a path. Shortly afterwards, TR on a grassy track.

3 1:30: A few minutes later, keep SH at a junction, still heading SW. Head SW at further junctions. Approaching **Highcliff Nab**, TR onto a path heading W along the escarpment. Soon, TL and descend steeply alongside a rock outcrop.

2 2:05: Go through a gate and TR. 35min later, TR at a junction on **Hutton Moor**.

1 2:35: Shortly afterwards, TL and head W on a path.

4 2:50: Reach a junction. To continue on **Stage 5b** (to climb Roseberry Topping), go through a gate and head W: alternatively, TL to head directly to **Kildale** on Stage 5a (avoiding Roseberry Topping). Descend to a saddle. Then climb a clear path heading up the slope of **Roseberry Topping**.

S 3:15: Arrive on the summit of **Roseberry Topping (320m)**. For **Stage 5a**, retrace your steps E back to 4: alternatively, to head to **Newton-under-Roseberry**, take one of the paths descending W from the summit: when you meet **Roseberry Lane**, head W to the **A173**.

W-E

Stage 5d: Skelton Green to Skelton

S From the junction, head N on a path. After 5-10min, TR on a lane. Shortly afterwards, TL, descending steps.

F 0:15: Reach **High Street** in **Skelton**.

Stage 5e: Skelton to Saltburn-by-the-Sea

S Head N on **Coniston Road**. Shortly afterwards, TR on **Derwent Road**. A few minutes later, TR on **Windermere Drive**. Keep SH onto **Hamsterley Way** and then **Bowland Road**.

1. 0:20: TR on a path between houses. Pass under the **A174**. A few minutes later, TR at a fork: easy to miss.

2. 0:35: Pass under **Saltburn Viaduct**. Shortly afterwards, TL at a complicated junction: take the broadest of the paths which climb N. Soon there are superb views of Saltburn Viaduct.

3. 0:45: Bear left up a tarmac lane. Shortly afterwards, TL up another lane. A few minutes later, TL up steps. Immediately afterwards, TR along a road.

F 1:00: Arrive in **Saltburn-by-the-Sea**: TL on **Dundas Street East** to head into town or keep SH for **Stage 6a**.

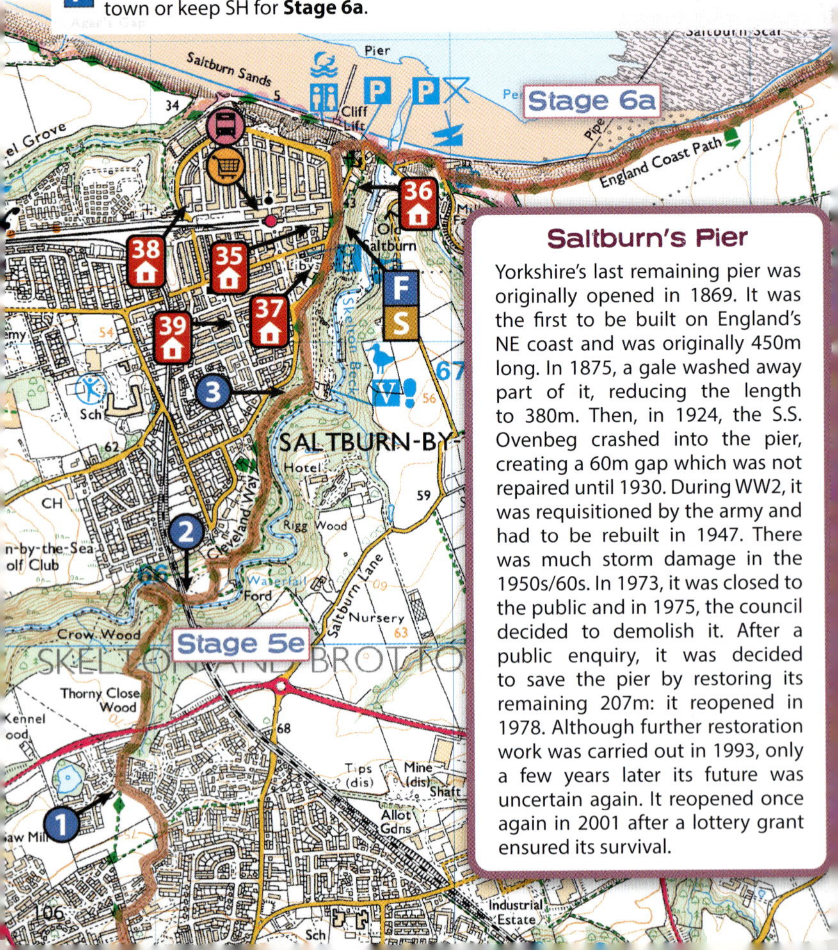

Saltburn's Pier

Yorkshire's last remaining pier was originally opened in 1869. It was the first to be built on England's NE coast and was originally 450m long. In 1875, a gale washed away part of it, reducing the length to 380m. Then, in 1924, the S.S. Ovenbeg crashed into the pier, creating a 60m gap which was not repaired until 1930. During WW2, it was requisitioned by the army and had to be rebuilt in 1947. There was much storm damage in the 1950s/60s. In 1973, it was closed to the public and in 1975, the council decided to demolish it. After a public enquiry, it was decided to save the pier by restoring its remaining 207m: it reopened in 1978. Although further restoration work was carried out in 1993, only a few years later its future was uncertain again. It reopened once again in 2001 after a lottery grant ensured its survival.

E-W

Stage 5e: Saltburn-by-the-Sea to Skelton

F From the E end of **Dundas Street East**, head S on a road. Soon TL onto **Glenside**, heading S. 5min later, TL down steps. A few minutes later, TR on a lane.

3 0:15: Shortly afterwards, keep SH at a junction. After a while, there are superb views of Saltburn Viaduct. Shortly afterwards, TR at a complicated junction.

2 0:25: Pass under **Saltburn Viaduct**. Pass under the **A174**. Then follow a path between houses.

1 0:40: TL on **Bowland Road**. Keep SH onto **Hamsterley Way** and then **Windermere Drive**. TL on **Derwent Road**. TL on **Coniston Road**.

S 1:00: Reach **High Street** in **Skelton**.

Stage 5d: Skelton to Skelton Green

F From **High Street**, head S on a road. Soon pick up a path. TR briefly along **Swilly Lane**. Shortly, TL and head S on a path.

S 0:15: Reach a junction on the main road at **Skeleton Green**.

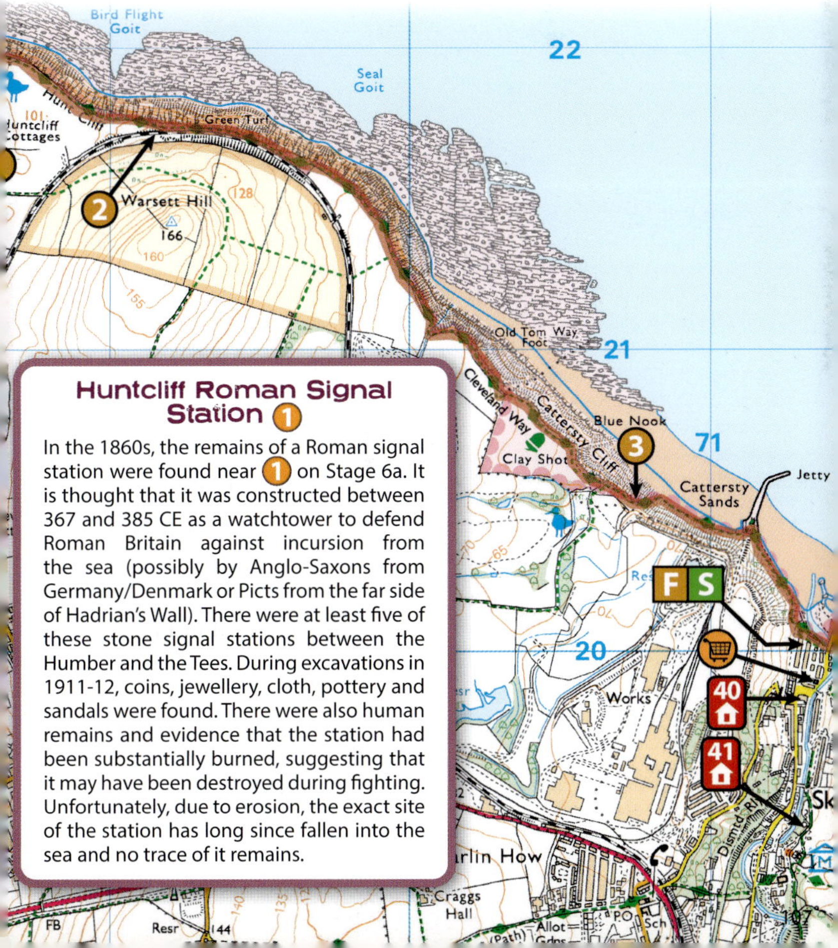

Huntcliff Roman Signal Station 1

In the 1860s, the remains of a Roman signal station were found near 1 on Stage 6a. It is thought that it was constructed between 367 and 385 CE as a watchtower to defend Roman Britain against incursion from the sea (possibly by Anglo-Saxons from Germany/Denmark or Picts from the far side of Hadrian's Wall). There were at least five of these stone signal stations between the Humber and the Tees. During excavations in 1911-12, coins, jewellery, cloth, pottery and sandals were found. There were also human remains and evidence that the station had been substantially burned, suggesting that it may have been destroyed during fighting. Unfortunately, due to erosion, the exact site of the station has long since fallen into the sea and no trace of it remains.

6 Saltburn-by-the-Sea/ Staithes

For W-E trekkers, Saltburn marks the beginning of the journey along the Yorkshire coast and Section 6 is a magnificent introduction to this second phase of the CLW. Shortly after leaving Saltburn, you reach the top of the cliffs to be met by the first of the magnificent, far-reaching sea views that will accompany you for much of the rest of the trek. A grassy path leads you along the coast through Hunt Cliff Nature Reserve, passing the site of a Roman Signal Station (see p107) and a trio of lovely sculptures by Richard Farrington which are perched magnificently on the cliff edge (see p112). Although the route returns to sea level as it passes through the village of Skinningrove, the path soon rises again, crossing the highest point on England's E coast as it makes its way to Boulby and Staithes. You will pass the alum quarries of Loftus and Boulby which provide evidence of the region's industrial past and fortunately, they only have a minor impact on Section 6's aesthetics.

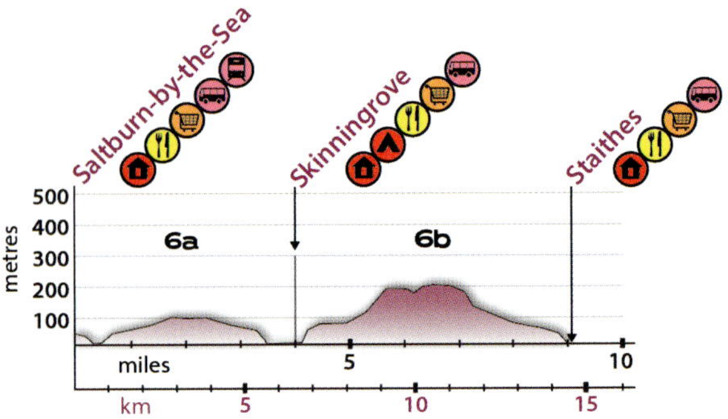

Boulby & Staithes viewed from the coast path (Stage 6b)

W-E trekkers finish at the picture-postcard village of Staithes: this jumble of red-roofed, whitewashed cottages is squeezed into a beautiful bay beneath the cliffs. As well as a few places to stay and eat, there are grocery shops where you can stock up on supplies. It is one of the loveliest settlements on the trek so book well in advance if you want to spend the night there.

For E-W trekkers, this remarkable part of the CLW, provides a wonderful finale to the coastal phase of the trek and the bars/restaurants of Saltburn ensure that there is ample opportunity to celebrate its completion. Saltburn is an enjoyable place to stop for the night: for further information, see p98.

Mid-section, the village of Skinningrove has seen better days and most trekkers prefer to push on to Staithes or Saltburn (depending upon direction of travel). However, Moonfleet Guesthouse is a pleasant place to stay and Magpie Wood serves campers well.

Section 6 uses clear paths and tracks which are easy to walk upon. There are frequent waymarks, so route-finding is largely straightforward.

		Time	Distance	Ascent W-E	Descent W-E
Stage 6a	Saltburn-by-the-Sea/Skinningrove	1:45	4.0miles 6.5km	308ft 94m	436ft 133m
Stage 6b	Skinningrove/ Staithes	2:30	5.1miles 8.2km	696ft 212m	696ft 212m

Accommodation

- **Saltburn-by-the-Sea (Stage 5e/6a):** hotels; B&B; guest house
- **Skinningrove (Stage 6a/6b):** Moonfleet Guesthouse
- **Boulby (Stage 6b):** Alum House Luxury B&B
- **Staithes (Stage 6b/7a):** pubs; B&B

Camping

- **Skinningrove (Stage 6a/6b; 0.3 miles OR):** Magpie Wood Caravans & Glamping

Refreshments/Food

- **Saltburn-by-the-Sea (Stage 5e/6a):** pubs; restaurants; cafés; take-aways
- **Skinningrove (Stage 6a/6b; 0.4 miles OR):** KasKane Café & Covells Bar
- **Staithes (Stage 6b/7a):** pubs; cafés

Supplies

- **Saltburn-by-the-Sea (Stage 5e/6a):** supermarket; pharmacy; shops; ATMs
- **Skinningrove (Stage 6a/6b):** Shiela's local shop
- **Staithes (Stage 6b/7a):** Chapel Yard Stores; Co-op supermarket; shops

Escape/Access

- **Saltburn-by-the-Sea (Stage 5e/6a):** train station; Arriva 3/X3/X3A/X4/X4A; Moorsbus M4
- **Skinningrove (Stage 6a/6b):** Arriva 5/5A
- **Boulby (Stage 6b):** Arriva X4/X4A
- **Staithes (Stage 6b/7a):** Arriva X4/X4A

'Circle' by the sculptor Richard Farrington (Stage 6a)

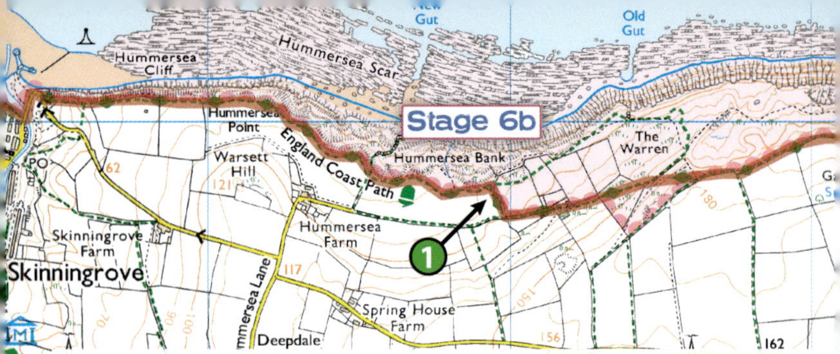

W-E

Stage 6a: Saltburn-by-the-Sea to Skinningrove

S The official route of the CLW heads down **Saltburn Road** to the coast. However, a more enjoyable option is to follow **Marine Parade** to the viewpoint above the beach where Saltburn's famous **water-balanced cliff lift** is located. From there, descend to the beach promenade using the steps or the cliff lift: this is the route that is marked on our map. TR along the promenade. Soon, pass to the right of the **Ship Inn**. Just afterwards, use a path to climb onto the cliffs. Head E on a path along the cliffs, following the coast through **Hunt Cliff Nature Reserve**.

1 0:45: Pass an information board near the site of a **Roman signal station** (see p107).

2 0:55: Pass '**Pillar**', the first of Richard Farrington's sculptures (see below). Nearby, you will also find '**Trawl Door**', the second sculpture: it is concealed from the path and is easy to miss. Continue E and soon you will reach '**Circle**', the third sculpture.

3 1:30: TL at an information board and descend steps towards the beach. Walk along the dunes at the top of the beach. Pass through a gap in a jetty.

F 1:45: Arrive in **Skinningrove** where you will find the '**Repus**' (see p113).

Richard Farrington's Sculptures 2

Near the edge of the cliffs along Stage 6a, you will find three interesting sculptures by the London born sculptor, Richard Farrington. They were originally made in 1990 using steel from the mill at nearby Skinningrove. '**Pillar**', the most westerly of the three, is a post attached to which are four linked symbols which represent sky, earth, air and sea.

Close by, but slightly harder to locate from the path, you will find '**Trawl Door**'. A trawl door is a large metal plate which is attached to the mouth of a trawler's net to keep the net open underwater. The sculpture was based on a trawl door that Farrington spotted in Whitby and the objects inside represent the trawler's catch.

'**Circle**', the most easterly sculpture, is most people's favourite. It represents a giant charm bracelet: each of the 10 charms hanging from it symbolise something of local significance. The horse, for example, represents the Cleveland Bay horse (a local breed). In fact, the sculpture that you see today is not the original. In 1996, vandals cut the first sculpture from its mount and rolled it off the cliff and into the sea. The frame and mount of the replacement sculpture were manufactured more robustly to deter vandals. Some of the original charms were found on the beach and reused in the new sculpture.

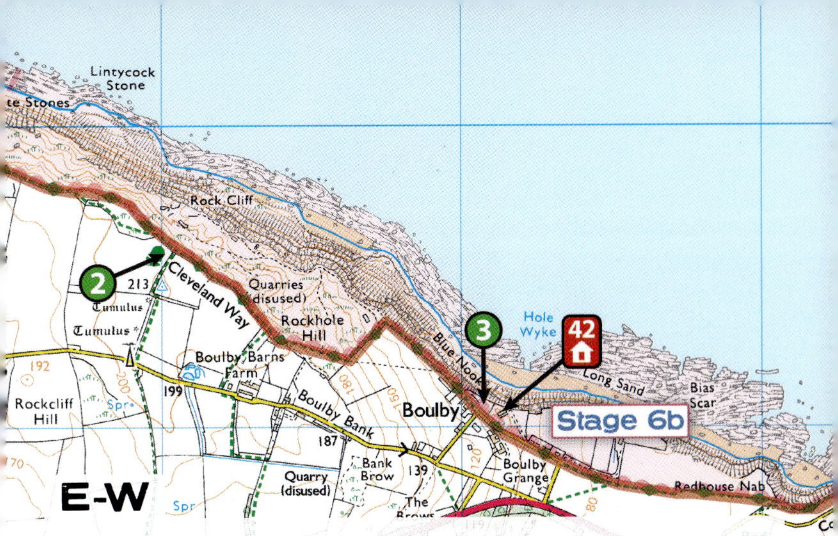

Stage 6a: Skinningrove to Saltburn-by-the-Sea

F From **Skinningrove**, head NW. Pass through a gap in a jetty. Then walk along the dunes at the top of the beach. Soon, TL and climb steps onto the cliffs.

3 0:15: Head NW on a path along the cliffs. After a while, pass '**Circle**', the first of Richard Farrington's sculptures (see p112).

2 0:50: Pass '**Trawl Door**', the second sculpture: it is concealed from the path and is easy to miss. If you reach the nearby '**Pillar**', the third sculpture, then you have already passed Trawl Door.

1 1:00: Pass an information board near the site of a **Roman signal station** (see p107). Continue W on a path along the cliffs through **Hunt Cliff Nature Reserve**. Descend to a road beside the **Ship Inn**: TR and head W along the beach promenade. The official route of the CLW winds up **Saltburn Road** to **Saltburn-by-the-Sea**. However, a more enjoyable option is to leave **Saltburn Road** at the first hairpin and climb steps to the viewpoint above the beach (beside Saltburn's **water-balanced cliff lift**): this is the route that is marked on our map. Alternatively, take the cliff lift (which departs from the base of the pier). From the viewpoint, head S alongside **Marine Parade** and then **Saltburn Road**.

S 1:45: Arrive in **Saltburn-by-the-Sea**: TR on **Dundas Street East** to head into town or keep SH for **Stage 5e**.

The Repus F

The Repus is an old fishing 'coble' that was owned by a fisherman from Skinningrove who died in the 1980s. The boat was restored and placed on the shore of the village of Skinningrove (Stage 6a/6b) as a memorial to those who died at sea. Two carved wooden figures were placed in the boat, one at the tiller and the other in the bow. Unfortunately, at the time of writing, the boat was in need of further restoration.

Boulby Alum Quarries 2

Alum is a chemical that is used to fix dyes to textiles. In Britain, it was manufactured by processing shale. The alum industry was Britain's first chemical industry. There are approximately 50 alum sites in England, most of which were along the Yorkshire coast. The Boulby alum works were one of the most productive. They were founded in the 1650s by the Conyers family of Boulby Manor. The nearby hamlet of Boulby was built for the alum workers. The works operated until 1871.

W-E

Stage 6b: Skinningrove to Staithes

S From the **Repus**, continue E along the seafront past a row of cottages. Near a toilet block, TL, cross a bridge and head N on **Beach Road**. A few minutes later, TL onto a path and climb onto **Hummersea Cliff**.

1 0:40: Keep on the path when it bends right (ignoring a path descending to the left). A few minutes later, TL up a track. Just after a house, continue on a path. Soon notice the bleak expanse of the **Loftus alum quarries** below the path.

2 1:25: Pass a **trig point** (just S of the path), marking the highest point on England's E coast. The **Boulby alum quarries** (see p113) are just below to the N.

3 1:45: At **Boulby**, keep SH down a lane. Pass **Alum House Luxury B&B**. Soon, keep SH on a path alongside a field. A few minutes later, pass the '**Miners Bait Table**', a sculpture which doubles up as a picnic bench: it provides lots of information about the nearby Boulby potash mine.

4 2:20: TL along **Cowbar Lane**. Cross a bridge over **Staithes Beck** and enter the village of **Staithes**.

F 2:30: Arrive at **Main Street** in **Staithes**.

E-W

Stage 6b: Staithes to Skinningrove

F From **High Street**, descend NW to **Staithes Beck**. Cross a bridge. Shortly afterwards, TL along **Cowbar Lane**.

4 0:15: TR onto a lane and head W. After a while, pass the '**Miners Bait Table**', a sculpture which doubles up as a picnic bench: it provides lots of information about the nearby Boulby potash mine. A few minutes later, keep SH on a lane. Pass **Alum House Luxury B&B**.

3 0:50: Shortly afterwards, when the lane bends left, keep SH and climb on a path. The **Boulby alum quarries** (see p113) are just below to the N.

2 1:10: Pass a **trig point** (just S of the path), marking the highest point on England's E coast. Continue W and soon pass the bleak expanse of the Loftus alum quarries below the path. Later, at a house, keep SH down a track. Soon, TR down a path.

1 1:55: A few minutes later, stay on the path when it bends left (ignoring a path descending to the right). Later, descend to the shore: head S along **Beach Road**. Cross a bridge. Then TR near a toilet block.

S 2:30: Arrive at the '**Repus**' on the seafront in **Skinningrove** (see p113).

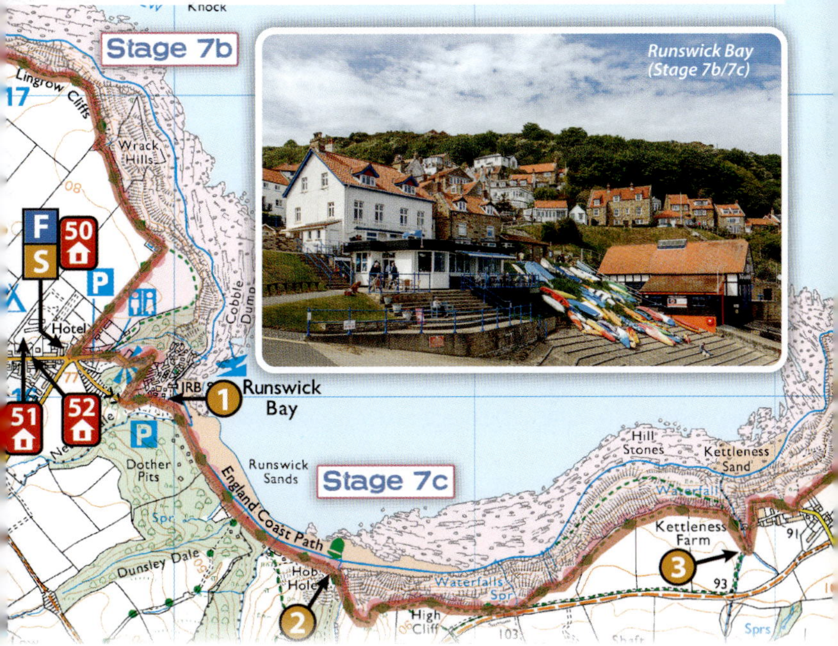

Runswick Bay (Stage 7b/7c)

7 Staithes/Whitby

This is another wonderful section of the Yorkshire coast with plenty more far-reaching sea views. For W-E trekkers any sorrow at leaving Staithes quickly dissipates as you climb once again onto the spectacular cliffs. The route is again punctuated by coves and charismatic villages: the lovely Runswick and Sandsend are right on the route of the CLW and are great places to take a break. However, the historic port town of Whitby, at the E extremity of Section 7, definitely steals the show.

The history of Whitby is so rich that we can scarcely do it justice here but it is fair to say that the sea played a leading part in the shaping of the town. Whitby is where the River Esk (which splits the settlement in two) meets the sea. The mouth of the river is flanked on both sides by high cliffs creating a natural harbour which provides excellent shelter for boats from the wind and waves that batter the shore. Consequently, Whitby was destined to become a port and much of its wealth was derived from fishing, whaling and marine trade. Later, after the arrival of the railway in the Victorian era, the town found fame as a seaside resort.

Just W of Whitby, you follow the line of the beach, passing interesting sculptures, the elegant Royal Crescent and countless multi-coloured beach huts. On the West Cliffs, above the town, you will find the fabulously located memorial to Captain Cook (the famous mariner who learnt his trade in the town; see p103) and pass through the Whale Bone Arch (made from the jawbones of a blue whale). From there, you can clearly see the ruins of Whitby Abbey (behind St Mary's church) on the cliffs on the E side of the river: the route of Section 8 passes the abbey and church.

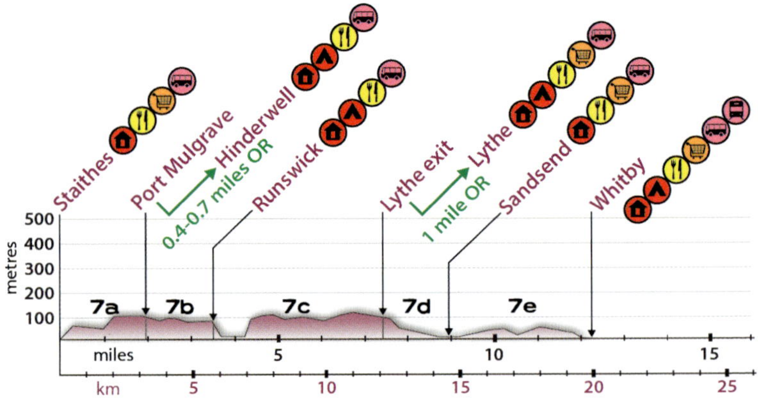

Of the many historic buildings in the town, one of the most interesting is the 17th century house where Captain Cook lived as an apprentice. It now houses the fascinating Captain Cook Memorial Museum which chronicles Cook's life using maps, papers, paintings and other exhibits: see **www.cookmuseumwhitby.co.uk**. Less organised, but equally fascinating, is the Whitby Museum and Pannett Art Gallery (**www.whitbymuseum.org.uk**): it was founded in 1823 to house fossils found in the nearby alum works and interesting items brought from around the world by Whitby's ships. The Whitby Lifeboat Museum (at the N end of Pier Road) is also worth a visit. Set in an old lifeboat station, it is packed with equipment, paintings, photos and mementos from famous wrecks and rescues: see **www.rnli.org**.

There is so much to see in Whitby that most trekkers prefer to stop for the night. However, it is not just walkers who visit: on sunny days, the town is thronged with holidaymakers. Fortunately, Whitby is also packed with places to stay and eat and has plenty of shops for resupply. As an old fishing port, it is renowned for its fish and scampi: a few of the restaurants serve some of the best fish and chips that you will find in England.

E-W trekkers finish Section 7 at the lovely village of Staithes which has a few grocery shops, pubs and accommodation options. Because it is one of the loveliest settlements on the trek, you should book well in advance. Mid-section, there is accommodation at Runswick and Sandsend (which are along the route of the trek) and Hinderwell and Lythe (which are a short distance OR).

Section 7 uses clear paths and tracks which are easy to walk upon. There are frequent waymarks, so route-finding is largely straightforward.

		Time	Distance	Ascent W-E	Descent W-E
Stage 7a	Staithes/ Port Mulgrave	1:00(W-E) 0:45(E-W)	1.9miles 3.0km	335ft 102m	33ft 10m
Stage 7b	Port Mulgrave/ Runswick Bank Top	0:30	1.6miles 2.6km	92ft 28m	144ft 44m
Stage 7c	Runswick Bank Top/ Lythe exit	1:45	3.9miles 6.2km	482ft 147m	440ft 134m
Stage 7d	Lythe exit/ Sandsend	0:30(W-E) 0:45(E-W)	1.5miles 2.4km	23ft 7m	289ft 88m
Stage 7e	Sandsend/Whitby	1:30	3.4miles 5.5km	210ft 64m	220ft 67m

Accommodation

- **Staithes (Stage 6b/7a):** pubs; B&B
- **Hinderwell (Stage 7a/7b; 0.4 miles OR):** St Hilda's Complex
- **Runswick Bank Top (Stage 7b/7c):** Runswick Bay Hotel; Runswick Bay Caravan & Camping Park; The Firs Guesthouse
- **Lythe (Stage 7c/7d; 1 mile OR):** The Stiddy pub
- **Sandsend (Stage 7d/7e):** hotels; B&B
- **Whitby (Stage 7e/8):** hotels; B&Bs; pubs. In addition to the properties marked on our maps, Discovery Accommodation run a series of guesthouses: book at www.discoveryaccommodation.com

Camping

- **Hinderwell (Stage 7a/7b; 0.6 miles OR):** Serenity Camping
- **Runswick Bank Top (Stage 7b/7c):** Runswick Bay Caravan & Camping Park
- **Lythe (Stage 7c/7d; 1 mile OR):** Lythe Caravan and Camping
- **Whitby (Stage 7e/8):** Folly Gardens Campsite

Refreshments/Food

- **Staithes (Stage 6b/7a):** pubs; cafés
- **Hinderwell (Stage 7a/7b; 0.4-0.7 miles OR):** restaurant; pubs; fish & chip shop; tea room

Fields of rapeseed in spring (Stage 7d)

- **Runswick (Stage 7b/7c):** Runswick Bay Tea Garden; Runswick Bay Hotel; Royal Hotel; Tides Beach Café
- **Lythe (Stage 7c/7d; 1 mile OR):** The Stiddy pub
- **Sandsend (Stage 7d/7e):** pubs; café; take-away
- **Whitby (Stage 7e/8):** pubs, restaurants, cafés; take-aways

Supplies

- **Staithes (Stage 6b/7a):** Chapel Yard Stores; Co-op supermarket; shops
- **Lythe (Stage 7c/7d; 1 mile OR):** Lythe Community Shop (snacks/basic groceries)
- **Sandsend (Stage 7d/7e):** Sandsend Stores (groceries/snacks/drinks)
- **Whitby (Stage 7e/8):** supermarket; pharmacy; shops; outdoor stores; ATMs

Escape/Access

- **Staithes (Stage 6b/7a):** Arriva X4/X4A
- **Hinderwell (Stage 7a/7b; 0.6 miles OR):** Arriva X4/X4A
- **Runswick Bank Top (Stage 7b/7c):** Arriva X4/X4A
- **Lythe (Stage 7c/7d; 1 mile OR):** Arriva X4/X4A
- **Sandsend (Stage 7d/7e):** Arriva X4/X4A
- **Whitby (Stage 7e/8):** train station; Arriva X4/X4A/X93; Coastliner 840

W-E

Stage 7a: Staithes to Port Mulgrave (Hinderwell exit)

S Head SE along **High Street**. Just after the **Cod & Lobster pub**, TR and climb on **Church Street**: at the end of it, keep SH, climbing on a path. Soon the route bends to the left. Just after buildings, TL and head N back to the coast: head E on the coast path.

1 0:55: Keep SH along a road.

F 1:00: Reach a bend in the road: TL onto a path for **Stage 7b**. Alternatively, head SW on the road for **Hinderwell** (0.6 miles OR).

Stage 7b: Port Mulgrave (Hinderwell exit) to Runswick Bank Top

S From the bend in the road, head SE on the coast path.

F 0:30: Arrive at **Runswick Bay Hotel** at **Runswick Bank Top**.

Stage 7c: Runswick Bank Top to Lythe exit

S From **Runswick Bay Hotel**, head E along **Bank Top Lane**. Soon, keep SH past the **Cliffemount Hotel** (which was closed at the date of press): descend on a lane which soon bends right. Keep heading downhill until you reach the beach.

1 0:05: Reach **Tides Beach Café** at **Runswick Bay**. TR and walk along the beach: occasionally, during very high tides, passage is temporarily impeded.

2 0:20: TR and leave the beach, heading up a narrow gully (hard to locate). The path becomes better defined as you climb. Head E along **High Cliff**.

3 0:55: At **Kettleness Farm**, turn sharp left and go through a gate. Just afterwards, pass **Kettleness**.

F 1:45: Reach a junction: keep SH to start **Stage 7d** or TR for **Lythe**.

E-W

Stage 7c: Lythe exit to Runswick Bank Top

F From the junction, head W on the coast path.

3 0:50: Shortly after passing **Kettleness**, go through a gate and TR. Continue W on the coast path. After a while, descend into a narrow gully: the path becomes faint.

2 1:20: TL along **Runswick Sands**: occasionally, during very high tides, passage is temporarily impeded.

1 1:35: From **Runswick Bay**, climb W on a road. Shortly after a car park, TR at a junction: continue upwards until you reach **Cliffemount Hotel** (which was closed at the date of press). From there, head W along **Bank Top Lane**.

S 1:45: Arrive at **Runswick Bay Hotel** at **Runswick Bank Top**.

Stage 7b: Runswick Bank Top to Port Mulgrave (Hinderwell exit)

F From **Runswick Bay Hotel**, head NE. 5min later, TL along the coast path.

S 0:30: Arrive at a bend in a road: keep SH (N) along the road for **Stage 7a**. Alternatively, head SW on the road for **Hinderwell** (0.6 miles OR).

Stage 7a: Port Mulgrave (Hinderwell exit) to Staithes

F Head N along the road.

1 0:05: Keep SH on the coast path. Shortly before Staithes, TL and head S away from the coast. Near some buildings, TR. Soon the route bends to the right. Keep SH down **Church Street**.

S 0:45: Arrive at the **Cod & Lobster pub** in **Staithes**.

Whitby (Stage 7e/8)

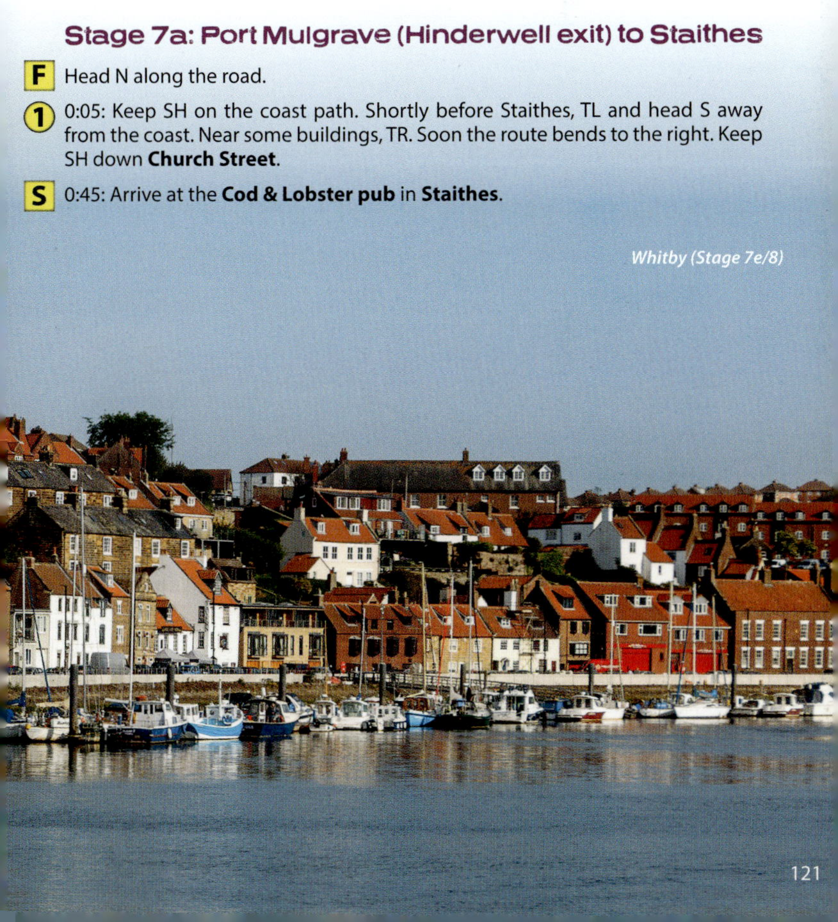

Sandsend (Stage 7d/7e)

Runswick Bay (Stage 7b/7c)

W-E

Stage 7d: Lythe exit to Sandsend

S From the junction, continue E along the cliffs.

1 0:15: Pass the site of **Deep Grove Alum Quarry**.

F 0:30: Arrive at **Sandsend**.

Stage 7e: Sandsend to Whitby

S Head SE along the promenade.

1 0:40: TL down a lane. 5-10min later, TR onto a path which climbs above the beach.

2 1:20: Reach the **Captain Cook Memorial** in **Whitby**. Pass though the famous **whale-bone arch**. Then descend steps: at the bottom, TL and walk down **Khyber Pass**. TR along **Pier Road**.

F 1:30: Arrive at **Whitby Swing Bridge**.

E-W

Stage 7e: Whitby to Sandsend

F Head N along **Pier Road**. TL up **Khyber Pass**. Soon, TR up steps.

2 0:15: Pass though the famous **whale-bone arch** at the **Captain Cook Memorial**. Then head W along the coast. 30min later, TL onto a lane.

1 0:50: TR along the **A174**.

S 1:30: Arrive at **Sandsend**.

Stage 7d: Sandsend to Lythe exit

F Head N along the promenade in **Sandsend**. Then follow a path N along the coast.

1 0:25: Pass the site of **Deep Grove Alum Quarry**.

S 0:40: Reach a junction: head W to start **Stage 7c** or TL for **Lythe**.

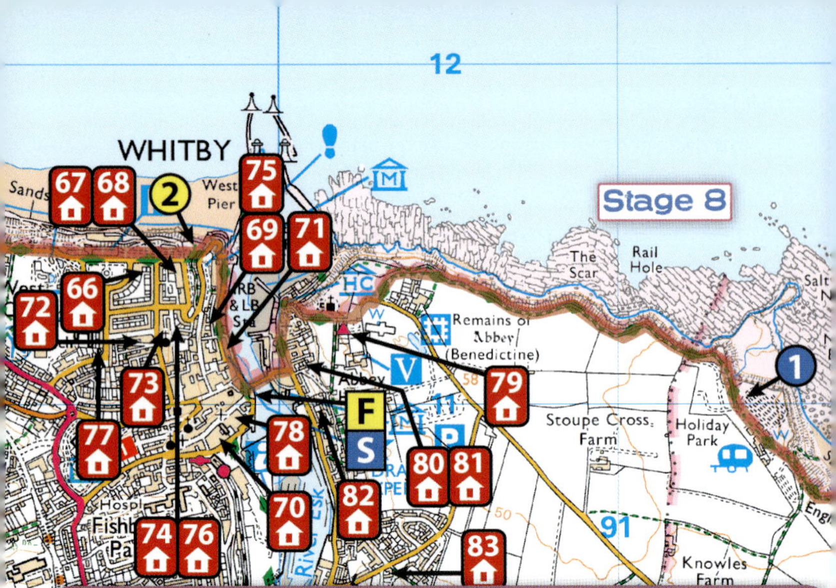

St Mary's Church

Situated on the E cliffs above Whitby, St Mary's Church is something of an architectural oddity: a fusion of different styles from different ages. It was founded around 1110 CE which probably explains the Norman appearance of the tower, nave and chancel. In later centuries, it was altered and extended but it was never completely rebuilt. It is thought that the north and south transepts were added in the 13th and 14th centuries. The battlements were added in the 16th century. Originally, the tower was taller but it became unstable and the top of it was removed in the 17th century. The church was extended in the 19th century and large windows were installed, allowing more light to enter.

The church's interior is one of the finest examples in England of an unaltered church with its pre-Victorian fittings intact: the galleries were installed between 1695 and 1818; the box pews and 3-decker pulpit date from 1778 (altered in 1847). The hearing trumpets on the pulpit date from 1843. The church graveyard was used as one of the settings in Bram Stoker's vampire novel, Dracula.

Whitby Abbey

Whitby Abbey is a fine example of English Gothic architecture and was founded in 657 CE by Hild, a nobleman's daughter, with the help of King Oswy of Northumbria. It served as a monastery for nuns and monks and quickly became a significant religious centre in the Anglo-Saxon world. In 664, it hosted the Synod of Whitby, a meeting which determined the mechanism to be used for working out the date of Easter (which we still use today).

It was abandoned in the 9th century after Viking invasion. In 1078, a new Benedictine community was established on the site and in the 13th century, the monastery church was rebuilt in the Gothic style. In 1539, the monastery was dissolved by Henry VIII: some of its stone was used in local buildings including the adjacent manor which now serves as a visitor centre. In 1914, during WW1, the German navy substantially damaged the abbey when it shelled Whitby. In 1920, it was donated to the Ministry of Works and today it is managed by English Heritage. The atmospheric location of the abbey inspired Bram Stoker to use it as a setting in his vampire novel, Dracula.

8 Whitby/ Robin Hood's Bay

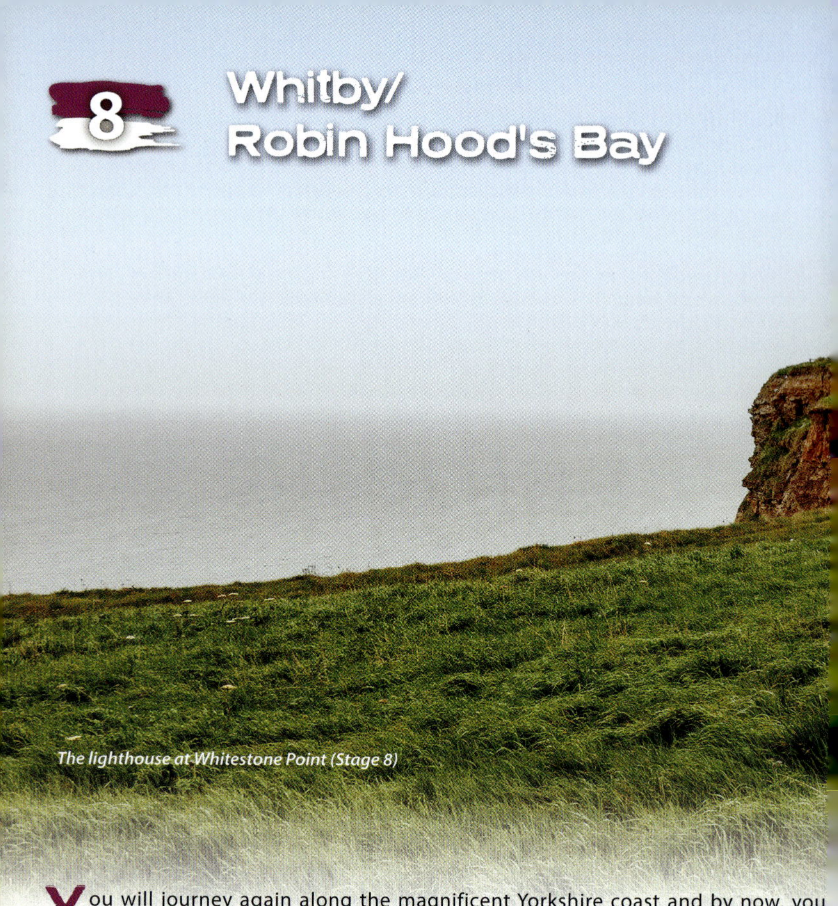

The lighthouse at Whitestone Point (Stage 8)

You will journey again along the magnificent Yorkshire coast and by now, you could be forgiven for thinking that the cliffs go on forever. In the unlikely event that you are tired of far-reaching sea views, there are other interesting sights to keep you occupied. On the cliffs above Whitby, take the time to visit St Mary's Church (see p124) which is just as much a museum as a place of worship. Next door, you will find the evocative ruins of Whitby Abbey (see p125). Because Section 8 is quite short, W-E trekkers should have time to take in some of Whitby's attractions before setting out and E-W trekkers could do that during the second half of the day.

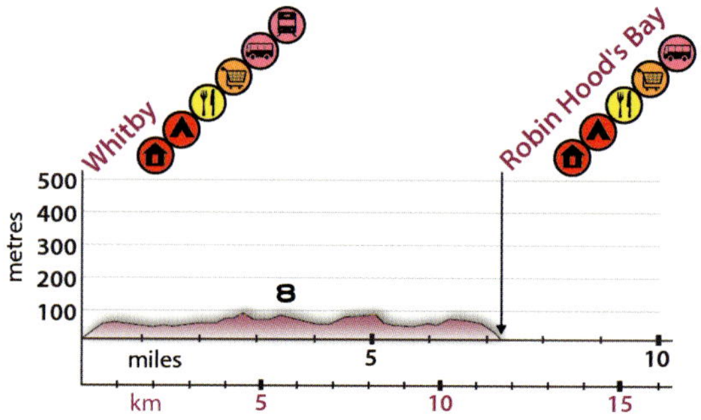

For W-E trekkers, the arrival into RHB (with its old stone buildings and winding streets) is wonderful. The section finishes at the Bay Hotel which has a superb beach-side location: it is a fabulous place to relax for a drink at the end of the day (if you can get a seat because this is also the finishing point of Wainwright's Coast to Coast Path and the bar is very busy). RHB's excellent facilities include hotels, B&Bs, campsites, restaurants, bars and shops. Most E-W trekkers will overnight at Whitby: see p116.

Section 8 uses clear paths and tracks which are easy to walk upon. There are frequent waymarks, so route-finding is largely straightforward.

		Time	Distance	Ascent W-E	Descent W-E
Stage 8	Whitby/ Robin Hood's Bay	3:30	7.3miles 11.8km	702ft 214m	722ft 220m

Accommodation

- **Whitby (Stage 7e/8):** hotels; B&Bs; pubs; In addition to the properties marked on our maps, Discovery Accommodation run a series of guesthouses: book at www.discoveryaccommodation.com
- **Robin Hood's Bay (Stage 8/9a):** hotels; B&Bs

Camping

- **Whitby (Stage 7e/8):** Folly Gardens Campsite
- **Robin Hood's Bay (Stage 8/9a):** Middlewood Farm Holiday Park; Hooks House Farm; Bay Ness Farm

Refreshments/Food

- **Whitby (Stage 7e/8):** pubs, restaurants, cafés; take-aways
- **Whitby Holiday Park (Stage 8):** Jet Bar and Bistro
- **Robin Hood's Bay (Stage 8/9a):** restaurants; pubs; cafés

The cliff path near RHB (Stage 8)

Supplies

- **Whitby (Stage 7e/8):** supermarket; pharmacy; shops; outdoor stores; ATMs
- **Robin Hood's Bay (Stage 8/9a):** Baytown Stores (groceries/sandwiches/snacks/drinks)

Escape/Access

- **Whitby (Stage 7e/8):** train station; Arriva X4/X4A/X93; Coastliner 840
- **Robin Hood's Bay (Stage 8/9a):** Arriva X93

W-E

Stage 8: Whitby to RHB

S Cross **Whitby Swing Bridge** and keep SH on **Bridge Street**. TL onto **Church Street**: at the end of it, climb the **199 steps**: the benches on the way up were originally built as a place to rest coffins while they were being carried upwards to the church. At the top, reach **St Mary's Church** (see p124). Just afterwards, continue on a road past **Whitby Abbey** (see p125). Shortly afterwards, TL and follow the coast path.

1 0:35: Keep SH through **Whitby Holiday Park**. Then continue E on the cliff path: do not descend to **Saltwick Bay**.

2 1:05: At **Whitestone Point**, pass **Whitby Fog Signal Station** with its huge fog horns on the roof. Shortly afterwards, the path passes to the right of a lighthouse.

3 1:50: Cross a bridge at **Maw Wyke Hole**. Then climb and continue along the cliff path.

4 3:10: Shortly after **Rocket Post Field** (see below), the route has been permanently diverted inland: TR and follow waymarks.

5 3:20: TL down **Station Road**. Pass **Baytown Stores**. Follow CLW signs down through winding streets into **Robin Hood's Bay**.

F 3:30: Reach the slipway by the beach in **Robin Hood's Bay**.

E-W

Stage 8: RHB to Whitby

F From the beach in **RHB**, climb N through the winding streets. Continue N on **Station Road**: keep SH past **Baytown Stores**.

5 0:20: TR on **Mount Pleasant N**.

4 0:30: TL and head NE along the coast. Soon go through **Rocket Post Field** (see below).

3 1:50: Cross a bridge at **Maw Wyke Hole**. Then continue NW along the cliff path.

2 2:35: Shortly after passing a lighthouse, reach **Whitby Fog Signal Station** with its huge fog horns on the roof. Continue NW along the coast.

1 3:05: Keep SH through **Whitby Holiday Park**. At **Whitby Abbey** (see p125), TR on a lane. Shortly afterwards, pass **St Mary's Church** (see p124) and descend the **199 steps**: the benches on the way down were originally built as a place to rest coffins while they were being carried up to the church. At the bottom of the steps, keep SH on **Church Street** which soon bends left. TR on **Bridge Street**.

S 3:30: Shortly afterwards, reach **Whitby Swing Bridge**.

4 Rocket Post Field

Many a ship fell victim to the rocks off Ness Point, just N of RHB. Between 1881 and 1931, RHB had its own lifeboat service which rescued 91 people over the years. Rocket Post Field was used to practise cliff rescues. Rockets carrying a thin line were fired to ships from posts (like the replica one that you see today). The crew of the ship caught the thin line and used it to pull a heavier rope over to the ship. A 'breeches buoy' was sent to the ship using the heavier rope: this was a lifebuoy with a pair of shorts attached that sailors could climb into. The breeches buoy was then pulled back to shore carrying the sailors. In 1936, some of the crew of the Heatherfield (a steam ship) were saved in this way including the captain who was carrying his canary in its cage.

Robin Hood's Bay

Rocket Post Field (Stage 8)

9 Robin Hood's Bay/ Scarborough

Between RHB and Scalby Mills (on the outskirts of Scarborough), the scenery is a delight. The path skirts the grassy edges of the cliffs with little to obscure the wonderful sea views other than colourful hedgerows of broom and gorse. Although this section is long and tiring, a few places of interest provide opportunities to take a break from walking. Just W of Ravenscar you will find the fascinating ruins of Peak Alum Quarries: this is the best place on the trek to learn about the alum industry which dominated the region in times gone by. Although few of the buildings are intact, what remains has been well-preserved and helpful information boards enable you to understand the processes that took place on the site. It is a rather beautiful place for an alum quarry and a lovely place to rest up.

Ravenscar itself has some interesting history too: in 1885, some local businessmen hatched a plan to build a new seaside resort here and spent a fortune buying land and building roads, water-mains and sewers. Unfortunately, however, Ravenscar's site was not ideal for a large new resort: trains struggled to climb the area's steep hills; the high cliff-tops were regularly battered by the high winds coming off the North Sea; and the beach was not ideal for holidaymakers because it is rocky and is a long way below the cliff-top settlement. In fact, only a few of the plots sold and the project ran out of money.

E of Ravenscar, you will pass Ravenscar Radar Station (see p137) which was used in WW2 to detect incursion by enemy aircraft/ships. The exteriors of a few of the structures are practically intact and the information boards explain what the buildings were used for.

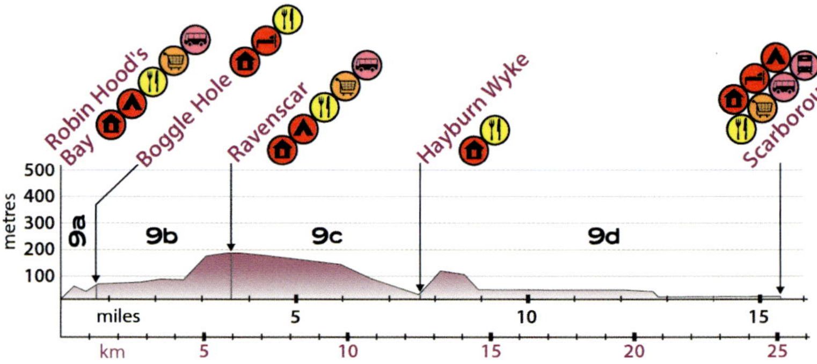

Ravenscar viewed from Peak Alum Quarries (Stage 9b)

E-W trekkers will have the wonderful RHB to look forward to at the end of the day, however, W-E trekkers will finish at South Bay in Scarborough (which is the largest town on the trek). It is a relief that the CLW sticks to the coast (following the pleasant promenade around the large sandy beaches of North Bay and South Bay) and avoids the parts of the town which are quite run down. However, on a sunny summer day, the seafront can be packed with holidaymakers and many trekkers will prefer to pass through without stopping for the night. If you do intend to stay overnight, then you might prefer to choose accommodation close to the seafront (although prices there tend to be a little higher): South Bay is probably the better choice because it has plenty of restaurants and shops. If you are inclined to spend some time in Scarborough itself then, other than beaches and water-parks, the attractions include Scarborough Sealife Centre, Scarborough Castle, the Rotunda Museum of Coastal Heritage and Geology and Scarborough Art Gallery.

If you are keen to avoid a night in Scarborough, then you could stay at Hayburn Wyke Inn (Stage 9c/9d; 0.3 miles OR). The following day, W-E trekkers would walk all the way from Hayburn Wyke to Filey (16 miles) or stop at Cayton.

Along the route of the trek, there is also accommodation at YHA Boggle Hole (Stage 9a/9b) and Ravenscar (Stage 9b/9c). A short distance OR from Stage 9d, you can stay at the pubs at Cloughton and Burniston.

Section 9 uses clear paths and tracks which are easy to walk upon. There are frequent waymarks, so route-finding is largely straightforward.

		Time	Distance	Ascent W-E	Descent W-E
Stage 9a	Robin Hood's Bay/ Boggle Hole	0:15	0.7miles 1.1km	135ft 41m	98ft 30m
Stage 9b	Boggle Hole/ Ravenscar	1:30 (W-E) 1:15(E-W)	2.9miles 4.6km	692ft 211m	125ft 38m
Stage 9c	Ravenscar/ Hayburn Wyke	1:30 (W-E) 1:45(E-W)	4.1miles 6.6km	125ft 38m	650ft 198m
Stage 9d	Hayburn Wyke/ Scarborough	3:30	7.8miles 12.5km	427ft 130m	502ft 153m

Accommodation

- **Robin Hood's Bay (Stage 8/9a):** hotels; B&Bs
- **Boggle Hole (Stage 9a/9b):** Boggle Hole YHA
- **Ravenscar (Stage 9b/9c):** Raven Hall Country House Hotel
- **Hayburn Wyke Inn (Stage 9c/9d; 0.3 miles OR)**
- **Cloughton (Stage 9d; 1.2 miles OR):** The Blacksmiths Arms Inn
- **Burniston (Stage 9d; 1.3 miles OR):** The Oak Wheel pub
- **Scalby Mills (Stage 9d; 0.5 miles OR):** YHA Scarborough
- **Scarborough (Stage 9d/10a):** hotels; B&Bs; hostel

Camping

- **Robin Hood's Bay (Stage 8/9a):** Middlewood Farm Holiday Park; Hooks House Farm; Bay Ness Farm
- **Ravenscar (Stage 9b/9c):** Bent Rigg Farm (0.4 miles OR)
- **Scalby Mills (Stage 9d; 0.5 miles OR):** Scarborough Camping and Caravanning Club site

Refreshments/Food

- **Robin Hood's Bay (Stage 8/9a):** restaurants; pubs; cafés
- **Boggle Hole (Stage 9a/9b):** Boggle Hole YHA
- **Ravenscar (Stage 9b/9c):** Ravenscar Visitor Centre (snacks/drinks); Ravenscar Tea Rooms; Raven Hall Country House Hotel
- **Hayburn Wyke Inn (Stage 9c/9d; 0.3 miles OR)**
- **Cloughton (Stage 9d; 1.2 miles OR):** The Blacksmiths Arms Inn
- **Burniston (Stage 9d; 1.3 miles OR):** The Oak Wheel pub
- **Scalby Mills (Stage 9d):** pub
- **Scarborough (Stage 9d/10a):** restaurants; pubs; cafés

The cliffs above Hayburn Wyke (Stage 9c)

Supplies

- **Robin Hood's Bay (Stage 8/9a):** Baytown Stores (groceries/sandwiches/snacks/drinks)
- **Ravenscar (Stage 9b/9c):** Bent Rigg Farm Shop (basic groceries; 0.4 miles OR)
- **Scarborough (Stage 9d/10a):** supermarkets; pharmacy; shops; outdoor stores; ATMs

Escape/Access

- **Robin Hood's Bay (Stage 8/9a):** Arriva X93
- **Ravenscar (Stage 9b/9c):** East Yorkshire Buses 115
- **Burniston (Stage 9d; 1.3 miles OR):** East Yorkshire Buses 115
- **Cloughton (Stage 9d; 1.2 miles OR):** East Yorkshire Buses 115
- **Scarborough (Stage 9d/10a):** train station; Arriva X93; Coastliner 840/843; East Yorkshire Buses 10/12/13/115/128; Moorsbus M3; Shoreline Suncruiser: Filey Flyer 555

W-E

Stage 9a: RHB to Boggle Hole

S From the **Smugglers Ale House** in **RHB**, climb on **Albion Road**. Continue upwards on **Flagstaff Steps** where there is an old marker stone. Shortly afterwards, TR at a junction and continue climbing wooden steps. Soon the path heads S along the cliffs.

F 0:15: Reach **Boggle Hole YHA**.

Stage 9b: Boggle Hole to Ravenscar

S Cross a bridge over **Mill Beck**. Shortly afterwards, cross a lane and climb steps. Head S along the coast.

1 0:15: At the top of a long set of steps, TL along a lane. 5min later, TL on a path.

2 0:50: TL at a junction and cross a bridge. Then cross a field. A few minutes later, reach **Peak Alum Quarries**: the fascinating ruins (with information boards) are extensive. The CLW passes to the N of the ruins and then heads S inland. Soon, TL and climb on a track. A few minutes later, TR on a path.

F 1:25: Arrive at **Ravenscar Visitor Centre**.

Stage 9c: Ravenscar to Hayburn Wyke

S Head SE up **Station Road**. Shortly afterwards, TL on a track. A few minutes later, TR and walk SE along the coast path. Shortly afterwards, pass a **rocket post**: see p130. Shortly after that, pass **Ravenscar Tea Rooms**.

1 0:30: Pass **Ravenscar Radar Station** (see p137).

2 1:25: Descend a long set of steep steps. Just after crossing a bridge over a stream, TR at a junction and climb: alternatively, TL to visit a little waterfall and a pebble beach (a few metres away).

F 1:30: Shortly afterwards, reach a junction: TL for **Stage 9d** or keep SH for the **Hayburn Wyke Inn Detour** (see p139).

E-W

Stage 9c: Hayburn Wyke to Ravenscar

F From the junction, head NE. Shortly afterwards, at another junction, keep SH and cross a bridge: alternatively, TR to visit a little waterfall and a pebble beach (a few metres away).

2 0:10: Reach the top of a long set of steep steps. Continue N along the coast.

1 1:10: Pass **Ravenscar Radar Station** (see below). Later, pass **Ravenscar Tea Rooms**. Shortly afterwards, pass a **rocket post**: see p130. Shortly after that, TL on a track. A few minutes later, TR onto **Station Road**.

S 1:45: Shortly afterwards, reach **Ravenscar Visitor Centre**.

Stage 9b: Ravenscar to Boggle Hole

F From **Ravenscar Visitor Centre**, head SW on a lane. 10min later, TR and descend N on a path. Soon bear left and pass to the N of **Peak Alum Quarries**: the fascinating ruins (with information boards) are extensive. At the far side of the ruins, head W.

2 0:25: Shortly afterwards, cross a bridge and TR at a junction. A few minutes after the ruins of an old pill box, TR on a lane.

1 1:00: A few minutes later, TR and descend a long set of steps. Continue N along the coast. Descend a second set of steps. Then cross a lane.

S 1:15: Shortly, cross a bridge over **Mill Beck** and reach **Boggle Hole YHA**.

Stage 9a: Boggle Hole to RHB

F Head N along the cliffs. As you approach RHB, descend **Flagstaff Steps**: at the bottom (where there is an old marker stone), TR on **Albion Road**.

S 0:15: Reach the slipway by the beach in **Robin Hood's Bay**.

1 Ravenscar Radar Station

The radar station was built around 1935. The building closest to the coast was a look-out post which was built to observe the busy shipping lanes during peacetime and to detect enemy ships/aircraft in WW2. Further inland are the communications hut and the transmitter/receiver block. In 1942, the site was taken over by the Royal Air Force and it was used by coastguards until 1972. It was renovated in 1999. You can walk around the ruins which have helpful information boards.

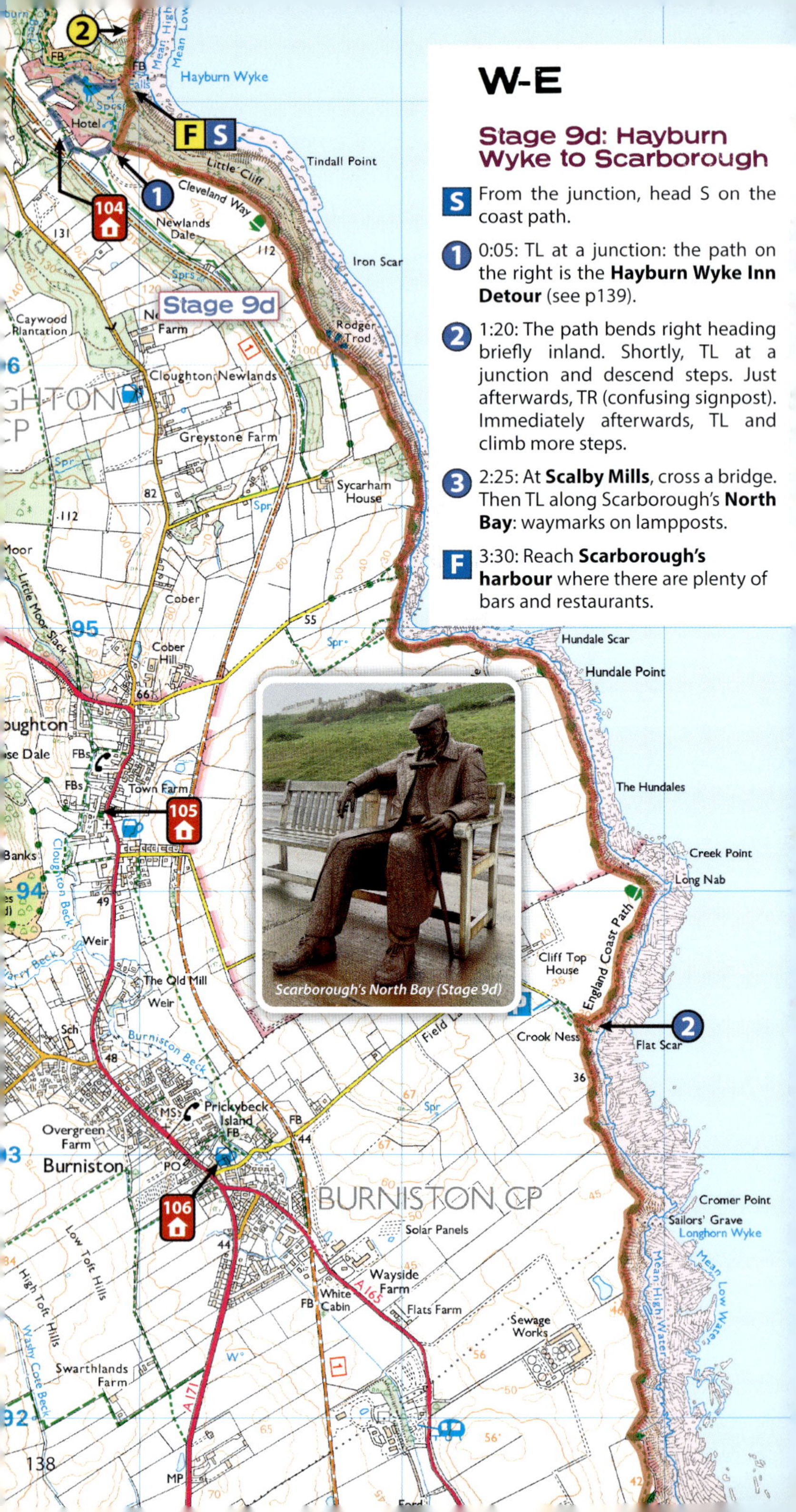

W-E

Stage 9d: Hayburn Wyke to Scarborough

S From the junction, head S on the coast path.

1 0:05: TL at a junction: the path on the right is the **Hayburn Wyke Inn Detour** (see p139).

2 1:20: The path bends right heading briefly inland. Shortly, TL at a junction and descend steps. Just afterwards, TR (confusing signpost). Immediately afterwards, TL and climb more steps.

3 2:25: At **Scalby Mills**, cross a bridge. Then TL along Scarborough's **North Bay**: waymarks on lampposts.

F 3:30: Reach **Scarborough's harbour** where there are plenty of bars and restaurants.

Scarborough's North Bay (Stage 9d)

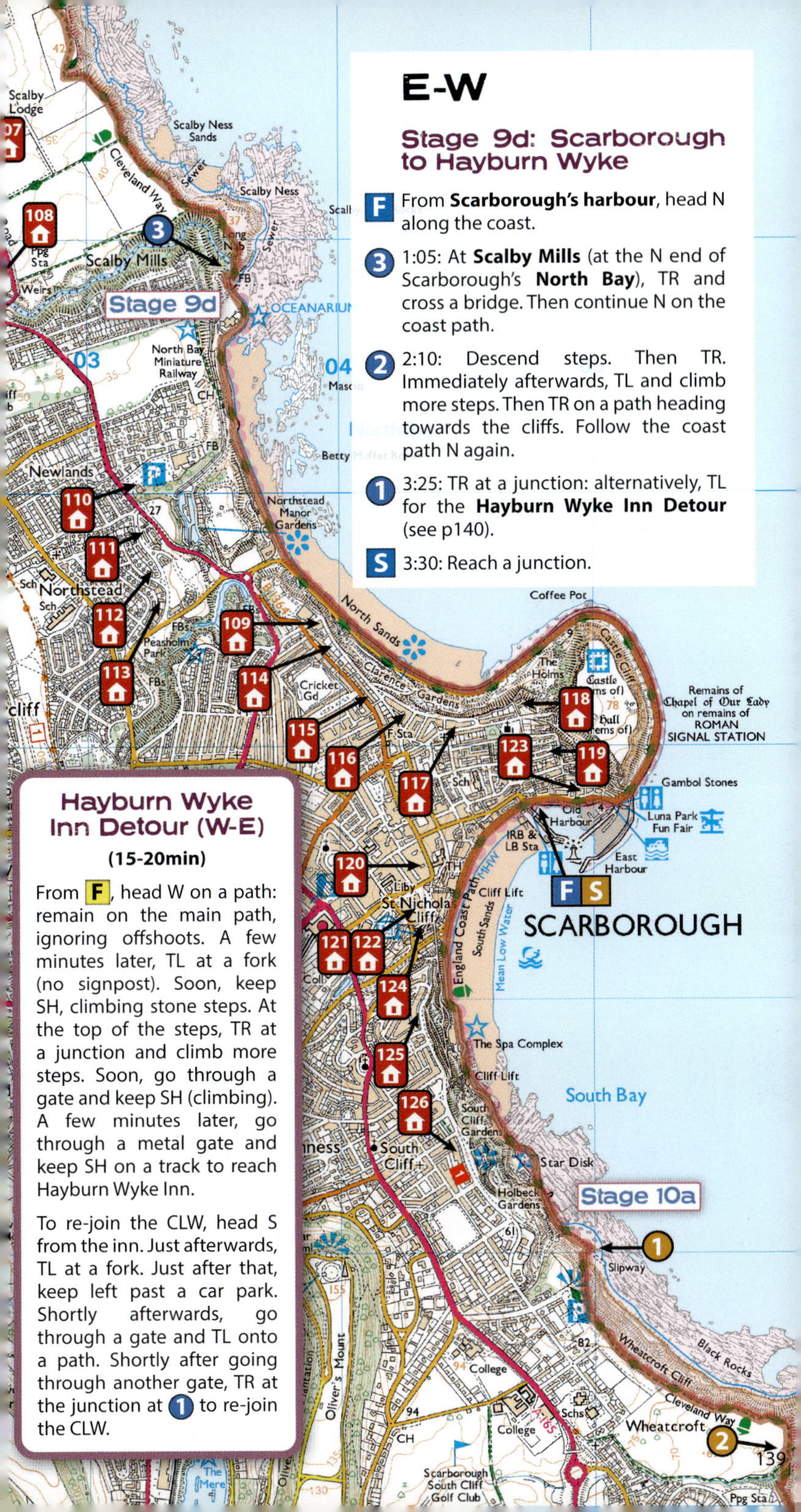

E-W

Stage 9d: Scarborough to Hayburn Wyke

F From **Scarborough's harbour**, head N along the coast.

3 1:05: At **Scalby Mills** (at the N end of Scarborough's **North Bay**), TR and cross a bridge. Then continue N on the coast path.

2 2:10: Descend steps. Then TR. Immediately afterwards, TL and climb more steps. Then TR on a path heading towards the cliffs. Follow the coast path N again.

1 3:25: TR at a junction: alternatively, TL for the **Hayburn Wyke Inn Detour** (see p140).

S 3:30: Reach a junction.

Hayburn Wyke Inn Detour (W-E)

(15-20min)

From **F**, head W on a path: remain on the main path, ignoring offshoots. A few minutes later, TL at a fork (no signpost). Soon, keep SH, climbing stone steps. At the top of the steps, TR at a junction and climb more steps. Soon, go through a gate and keep SH (climbing). A few minutes later, go through a metal gate and keep SH on a track to reach Hayburn Wyke Inn.

To re-join the CLW, head S from the inn. Just afterwards, TL at a fork. Just after that, keep left past a car park. Shortly afterwards, go through a gate and TL onto a path. Shortly after going through another gate, TR at the junction at **1** to re-join the CLW.

Hayburn Wyke Inn Detour (E-W)

(15-20min)

From the junction at 1, head W on a path. TR on a track and soon pass a car park. Shortly, afterwards, reach Hayburn Wyke Inn.

To re-join the CLW, head N from the inn on a track. Keep SH through a few gates. Descend steps. Then TL at a junction and descend more steps. Now head E at any junctions. Soon arrive at S where you re-join the CLW.

Robin Hood's Bay (Stage 8/9a)

B
Brambles Bistro

10 Scarborough/ Filey Brigg

Eastbound trekkers have one more beautiful coastal foray before reaching the end of the trek at the remote headland of Filey Brigg. The route out of Scarborough, along South Bay, is more enjoyable than the journey in: as you walk away from the harbour, the urban sprawl is left behind and sandy beaches and grassy cliffs stretch far into the distance. After passing Cayton Bay, you are on the home straight. The scenery is magnificent as you approach Filey Brigg, the site of an old Roman signal station and the CLW's E terminus: the chalk cliffs around Filey are home to the largest population of seabirds in the UK.

At the foot of Filey Brigg, however, your work is not done because, although you have completed the official route of the trek, you find yourself at an isolated stone bench in the middle of nowhere: to seek public transport or a celebratory drink, you will need to walk one more mile into the town of Filey. Furthermore, before heading back to civilisation, most people will want to stroll out onto the headland to enjoy the sublime coastal views one last time.

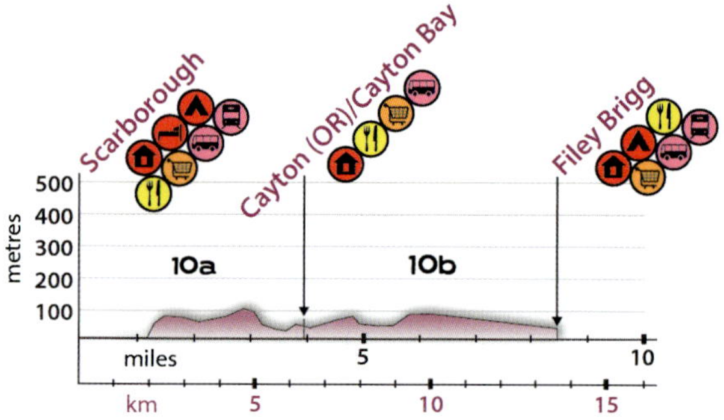

Approaching Filey Brigg (Stage 10b)

For E-W trekkers, the adventure is only beginning and Filey Brigg is a suitably spectacular place to get you in the mood for what is to come on the CLW's first five sections (along Yorkshire's amazing coastline). The wonderful scenery on Section 10 certainly whets your appetite but Scarborough is hardly the most inspiring place to spend your first night. For this reason, many E-W trekkers prefer to pass through the town and overnight at the Hayburn Wyke Inn (Stage 9c/9d; 0.3 miles OR): the downside is that this makes for a long first day. For further information on Scarborough, see p133.

Filey is a pleasant seaside town which has plenty of B&Bs and places to eat. For W-E trekkers, this makes it a great place to spend one last night on the trail. E-W trekkers could also overnight there before starting the trek the following morning. At the time of writing, the only available accommodation mid-section was at the Farrier in Cayton (1 mile OR): although there are plenty of campsites/caravan parks in Cayton Bay, we were unable to find one which would accept a booking for a single night.

Section 10 uses clear paths and tracks which are easy to walk upon. There are frequent waymarks, so route-finding is largely straightforward.

		Time	Distance	Ascent W-E	Descent W-E
Stage 10a	Scarborough/ Cayton exit	1:45	3.9miles 6.3km	472ft 144m	348ft 106m
Stage 10b	Cayton exit/ Filey Brigg	1:45	4.5miles 7.2km	246ft 75m	240ft 73m

Accommodation

- **Scarborough (Stage 9d/10a):** hotels; B&Bs; hostel
- **Cayton (Stage 10a/10b; 1 mile OR):** The Farrier
- **Filey (Stage 10b):** hotel; B&Bs

Camping

- **Filey (Stage 10b):** Filey Brigg Camping & Caravan Site; Centenary Way Camping and Caravan Park

Refreshments/Food

- **Scarborough (Stage 9d/10a):** restaurants; pubs; cafés
- **Cayton exit (Stage 10a/10b):** Lucy's Beach Shack (drinks/snacks)
- **Cayton (Stage 10a/10b; 1 mile OR):** pubs; restaurant; tea room
- **Filey (Stage 10b):** restaurants; pubs; cafés; take-aways

Supplies

- **Scarborough (Stage 9d/10a):** supermarkets; pharmacy; shops; outdoor stores; ATMs
- **Cayton (Stage 10a/10b; 1 mile OR):** grocery shops
- **Filey (Stage 10b):** supermarkets; pharmacy; shops; outdoor store; ATM

Escape/Access

- **Scarborough (Stage 9d/10a):** train station; Arriva X93; Coastliner 840/843; East Yorkshire Buses 10/12/13/115/128; Moorsbus M3; Shoreline Suncruiser: Filey Flyer 555
- **Cayton (1 mile OR)/Cayton exit (Stage 10a/10b):** East Yorkshire Buses 10/12/13; Shoreline Suncruiser: Filey Flyer 555
- **Filey (Stage 10b):** train station; East Yorkshire Buses 10/12/13; Shoreline Suncruiser: Filey Flyer 555

One of the many beaches along the CLW

W-E

Stage 10a: Scarborough to Cayton exit

S Head S along **South Bay**.

1 0:30: The path climbs away from the shore.

2 1:00: TR at a junction (the signpost is difficult to spot). A few minutes later, TL on a path.

3 1:20: TL along a road into **Osgodby**. 5min later, TL down steps.

F 1:45: Arrive at a junction near **Lucy's Beach Shack**: TR on a lane for **Cayton** or keep SH for **Stage 10b**.

Stage 10b: Cayton exit to Filey Brigg

S From the junction, head SE on a path.

1 0:35: Keep SH, ignoring a path climbing inland (no signposts). Continue SE along the coast path.

F 1:45: Arrive at the stone seat, at the foot of **Filey Brigg**, which marks the end of the trek. Congratulations! You have completed the CLW. Before you head into Filey, it is lovely to walk out onto Filey Brigg, a thin peninsula that juts out into the North Sea.

E-W

Stage 10b: Filey Brigg to Cayton exit

F From the stone seat, at the foot of **Filey Brigg**, head NW on a path along **North Cliff**.

1 1:10: Keep SH, ignoring a path climbing inland (no signposts). Continue NW along the coast path.

S 1:45: Arrive at a junction near **Lucy's Beach Shack**: TL on a lane for **Cayton** or keep SH for **Stage 10a**.

Stage 10a: Cayton exit to Scarborough

F From the junction, head NW on a path. Soon bear right towards the coast and follow a path along **Tenant's Cliff**. TR along a road into **Osgodby**.

3 0:25: TR, heading back towards the coast. Soon the path continues N along the cliffs. At **White Nab**, TR at a junction.

2 0:45: A few minutes later, TL on a path.

1 1:15: The path returns to the shore: head NW on the coast path. Continue N along Scarborough's **South Bay**.

S 1:45: Reach **Scarborough's harbour** where there are plenty of bars and restaurants.

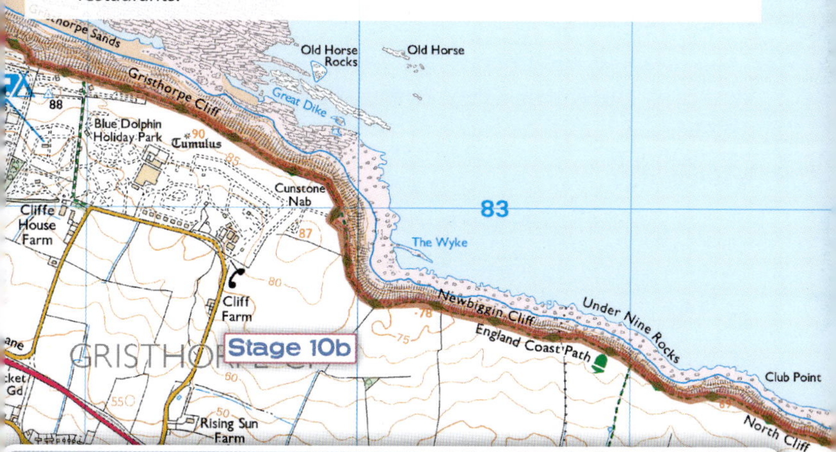

The stone seat at Filey Brigg marks the start/finish of the CLW

Walking between Filey Brigg and the village of Filey

(20-30min)

W-E

Although the CLW officially ends at Filey Brigg, you will need to walk into Filey (1 mile) to catch a bus/train: head S along the coast, following the route of the Yorkshire Wolds Way (another National Trail) which brings you to Filey's train station.

E-W

To get from the beach in Filey to the start of the CLW (1 mile), head N along the coast, following the route of the Yorkshire Wolds Way (another National Trail): this leads to the stone seat, at the foot of Filey Brigg, which marks the start of the trek.

The town of Filey

Saltburn-by-the-Sea (Stage 5e/6a)

KNIFE EDGE Outdoor Guidebooks

We thought guidebooks were boring so we decided to change them. Mapping is better than 40 years ago. Graphics are better than 40 years ago. Photography is better than 40 years ago. So why have walking guidebooks remained the same?

Well our guidebooks are **different**:

- **We use Real Maps.** You know, the **1:25,000/1:50,000** scale maps that walkers actually use to navigate with. Not sketch maps that get you lost. Real maps make more work for us but we think it is worth it. You do not need to carry separate maps and you are less likely to get lost so we save you time!
- **Numbered Waypoints** on our Real Maps link to the walk descriptions, making routes easier to follow than traditional text-based guidebooks. No more wading through pages of boring words to find out where you are! You want to look at incredible scenery and not have your face stuck in a book all day. Right?
- **Colour, colour, colour.** Mountains and cliffs are **beautiful** so guidebooks should be too. We were fed up using guidebooks which were ugly and boring. When planning, we want to be **dazzled** with full-size colour pictures of the **magnificence** which awaits us! So our guidebooks fill every inch of the page with beauty: big, **spectacular** photos of mountains, etc.
- **More practical size.** Long enough to have Real Maps and large pictures but slim enough to fit in a pocket.

Now all that sounds great to us but we want to know if you like what we have done. So hit us with your feedback: good or bad. We are not too proud to change.

Follow us for trekking advice, book updates, discount coupons, articles and other interesting hiking stuff.

www.knifeedgeoutdoor.com

info@knifeedgeoutdoor.com

@knifeedgeoutdoor

@knifeedgeout

@knifeedgeoutdoor

Facebook Groups

If you have any questions which are not answered in our books, then you can ask the author in one of our Facebook Groups. Any updates to our books are posted in the groups too.

The group for this book is **'The Cleveland Way'**. Join by scanning the QR code below or use the following URL: **www.facebook.com/groups/ClevelandWay**